BUSINESS LOBBIES

BUSINESS LOBBIES

The Public Good
& the Bottom Line

Sar A. Levitan
&
Martha R. Cooper

THE JOHNS HOPKINS UNIVERSITY PRESS
Baltimore and London

The Johns Hopkins University Press, Baltimore, Maryland 21218
The Johns Hopkins Press Ltd., London

Library of Congress Cataloging in Publication Data

Levitan, Sar A.
Business Lobbies

Includes bibliographical references and index.
1. Business and politics—United States.
2. Lobbying—United States. 3. Pensions—United States.
4. Insurance, Unemployment—United States. 5. Industrial
relations—United States. I. Cooper, Martha R.
II. Title.
JK467.L48   1984   322'.3'0973   83–48071
ISBN 0–8018–3108–3

Contents

Preface *vii*

I. COALITIONS TO WIN *1*

1. Mutual Interests *3*
Team Work *3*
For Better or Worse *10*

2. The Old Establishment *12*
Many Mansions *12*
National Association of Manufacturers *13*
Chamber of Commerce of the United States *17*
Attempted Merger and Persisting Differences *23*

3. Employer Associations in a Mixed Economy *27*
Peace-making with the Inevitable *27*
The Voice of Business Elites *29*
Small Business *40*
All in the Family *44*

4. Getting the Act Together *50*
New Tactics *50*
Supply Side Economics *52*
Constraints on the New Order *61*
Beyond Cupidity? *63*

II. IT PAYS TO DO HOMEWORK *65*

A Formidable Team *66*

5. Private Pension Issues: Locking the Barn
after the Horse Has Been Stolen *67*
The Stakes and the Players *69*
The Long Road to ERISA *70*
The ERISA Debate: Gradual Compromise *72*
Employer Strategy *77*
Business's Post-ERISA Predicament *80*
President's Commission on Pension Policy: Trying to Lock Up *82*

The Multiemployer Problem   *83*
ERISA Reform   *86*
Seizing the Initiative   *89*

6. Unemployment Insurance: Persistence Pays Off   *91*
The Players   *92*
The System   *94*
The Principles: Controlling the Agenda   *96*
The Issues   *97*
The 1965–66 Round: Employers Unite to Defeat Labor's Bill   *103*
The 1969–70 Round: Employers Score Again   *106*
Lost Ground: 1971–74   *107*
The 1975–76 Round: Cutting the Losses   *108*
The Cost-saving Crusade   *110*
The Outlook: 1983 and Beyond   *112*

7. Labor Law and Union Power: Employers Win Big   *115*
The Wagner Act   *116*
The First Four Decades   *117*
Common Situs Picketing: A Surprise Win   *119*
Labor Law Reform: Pulling Out the Stops   *122*
Labor-Management Standoff   *135*

8. Lobbying Lessons   *137*

Notes   *143*

Index   *151*

Preface

American business has always influenced legislative developments in Washington, but it is only in the past decade that business lobbies have learned to work together and invest sizable resources in Washington operations. In fact, a decade ago many of the major employer associations were not even located in the nation's capital. In 1964, Barry Goldwater failed to attract the support of many business leaders, and the momentum (both in terms of ideas and legislative track record) seemed to belong more to the backers of the Johnson administration's Great Society than to the business community.

Since the mid-1960s, however, the employer community has learned the costs of inactivity and has expanded its influence in the legislative process. A critical examination of business lobbies' agendas, philosophies, and strategies is now essential to an understanding of the formulation of federal social welfare legislation.

Perhaps following the old dictum "If you can't beat 'em, join 'em," many major corporate executives and numerous lesser lights were willing to make peace with the growing welfare state. To be sure, it was a love-hate relationship, and business executives pushed for government support if it helped their corporations while they tried to minimize the costs and impact of social programs designed to aid the poor and even the middle class. Government regulations could be burdensome, but the same law that imposed costly pension rights for corporate employees also helped establish a more stable work force and generated new markets for financial institutions and new sources for investment capital. On the macroeconomic level, the vast majority of business executives acknowledged the need for active fiscal and monetary policies to maintain a strong level of demand, moderate rates of unemployment, and social stability. In general, the job of the business lobbies was to make the best of a difficult situation.

However, as the 1970s progressed, business lobbies saw numerous opportunities to capture the legislative momentum. They became diligent students of the liberal-labor coalitions and learned their lessons well. By investing considerable money and effort, business advanced the art of coalition-building and succeeded in mounting an impressive grass-roots network.

Of course, this crusade was helped by the conservative drift of the American political scene. When President Reagan took office, the business community was offered the opportunity to help his administration roll back the advances made by the welfare state. Prior to the 1980 Republican convention, candidate Reagan had not been the first choice of America's corporate board rooms, but business leaders cast their lot with Reagan once the preferred candidates had dropped out of the race. Having identified themselves with the goals of the Reagan administration and having benefited from its actions, business coalitions based their future status in Washington and with the public upon the fortunes of Reagan's policies.

This study first delves into the workings and objectives of the major business lobbies in America. Although they rarely speak with one voice, employer organizations tend to act in unison on pressing issues or when the stakes are high, as they were in 1981. Aided by a skillful administration campaign, the business community was able to sell major parts of its agenda to the general public on the grounds that what is good for business is also good for the rest of America. Two years later, this selling job is becoming increasingly difficult because the business community has failed to deliver on the unrealistic promises made by the Reagan administration. The business community may find that the marriage they entered into in 1981 with the Reagan–New Right alliance is not easy to escape. In this case the public may not buy a "no fault" divorce.

The second part of this study contains three case studies that demonstrate the diversity of the lobbying landscape. The case study devoted to pension legislation shows the cost to employers when they fail to do their homework. The unemployment insurance case, on the other hand, shows how employers pragmatically organized to keep the program as lean and decentralized as possible. The business community understood the benefits of the new federalism long before it became a slogan. The analysis of common situs picketing and labor law reform shows how the business community won major battles against considerable odds by effectively mobilizing its resources.

Martha Cooper, who collaborated in preparing this study, left to pursue the study of law before the final draft was completed and should not be held responsible for all the conclusions. I am indebted to Richard Belous for his thoughtful and extensive contributions to Part I of this study and to Bobby Webster for the final touches in preparing the manuscript for publication.

For helpful criticism, I am also indebted to John Albertine of the American Business Conference; Jeffrey Joseph, Richard Rahn, and Michael Romig of the Chamber of Commerce of the United States; Robert Holland and Ken McLennan of the Committee for Economic Development; Randolph Hale and Alexander Trowbridge of the NAM; Herbert Liebenson of the National Small Business Association; John Post of the Business Roundtable; Karen Ferguson of the Pension Center; Eldred Hill of the UBA; Ken Klein and Robert Scheerschmidt of the Xerox Corporation; and Norman Ornstein of the American Enterprise Institute.

This study was prepared under a grant from the Ford Foundation to The George Washington University's Center for Social Policy Studies. In accordance with the Foundation's practice, responsibility for the content was left completely with me.

Sar A. Levitan

I
Coalitions
to Win

1

Mutual Interests

People of the same trade seldom meet together, even for mer-
riment and diversion, but the conversation ends in a conspiracy
against the public, or in some contrivance to raise prices.
—Adam Smith, *The Wealth of Nations*

Team Work

It is ironic that Adam Smith, often viewed as the patron saint of the business
community, showed such little respect for his admirers. But as later economists
noted, the champion of free markets and originator of the invisible hand
concept was not above suspecting the motives underlying the action of businessmen. Political economy, Smith realized, was much more than the simple
laws of supply and demand operating under perfect competition. Public policy
could not ignore the social and political rules of the game, an entire web of
institutions and cultural forces, and how those rules were enforced.[1] Before
supply and demand even took the field, the rules of the game had already been
made on the sidelines.

The various players in this economic game—employers, workers,
consumers—have always recognized this fact of life. In recent years, with
increasing intervention in and regulation of business activity by government,
the stakes have grown substantially. But individual players can accomplish
little to alter the rules or to reverse a particular call by the umpires. Even the
most powerful players—American Telephone and Telegraph Company or
International Business Machines Corporation—rarely shift the game to their
advantage by playing alone.

American folklore may emphasize rugged individualism and atomistic
competition, but the actual workings of our political economy have stressed
coalition-building and joint action. The railroads were built by barons of private
enterprise but not without prior governmental subsidies. And the early indus-

trialists not only depended upon governmental protection from foreign competition, but also fought for public policies encouraging the supply of cheap labor. Business, like labor, learned early the importance of working with the government in order to get favorable public programs enacted.

One of the most striking political changes in the past decade has been the increased effectiveness employer associations have demonstrated in their dealings with the rather formidable Washington policy establishment. The business community does not necessarily speak with one voice, however; it comprises a large diversity of interests. This is reflected in the proliferation of organizations in Washington presenting the views of business to federal policymakers on Capitol Hill, in the White House, and at the regulatory and executive agencies.

Companies have chosen different ways to influence the government depending on their goals and the resources at their disposal. A large company with multifaceted operations affected by government regulations in many fields—or a company of which the government is a major customer—may invest in a Washington office, hire one or more representatives to monitor the issue areas of its primary concern, and engage a well-connected Washington law firm to pursue its interests with the relevant agency bureaucrats. Businesses with fewer resources for lobbying will rely on the services of associations representing the common interests of their trade, industry, or sector, but not necessarily the specific needs of each firm. These are highly specialized organizations and general purpose business organizations. Many companies use all these channels; others are more selective. With so many organizations claiming to represent business's views, the policymaker who is trying to decipher what "business" thinks on a particular issue can become confused. In the past few years, however, business has gotten the knack of working together. This has come with the recognition both of what can be accomplished (within antitrust constraints) through the investment of resources in Washington, and of what is at stake if the investment opportunity is passed up.

Coalition Building

In the not too distant past, many business executives displayed little interest in federal operations, and most of them were not even located in the nation's capital. As Irving S. Shapiro, former chairman of DuPont and a leader of the Business Roundtable, put it: "A generation or two in the past, you could get by in business by following four rules: stick to business, stay out of trouble, join the right clubs, and don't talk to reporters." Today, however, he noted, "executives are realizing that the day is gone when the spot at the top of an organization chart permitted a private lifestyle."[2]

Employers asserted that they were losing control of their costs to government regulators who had no experience with meeting a payroll and no idea of entrepreneurial struggles in a competitive market. In the late 1960s and early 1970s, the laws and regulations emanating from Washington steadily raised the cost of doing business. It became apparent to American business leaders that in order to win in Washington, they would have to change the rules to their advantage; and that meant playing Washington's game.

Whatever representation the business community had in Washington seemed inadequate to meet the expanding impact of the federal government upon business affairs. Companies needed help to get a bigger slice of government outlays and to counteract the activities of the opposition—public interest law firms, unions, consumers, and minority groups. Employer representatives studied the methods of their opponents and, by using the wholly superior resources at their disposal, had little trouble surpassing the forces of the opposition and improving upon their tactics. They organized popular support, hired consultants, marshalled facts, learned to use the media, made alliances, filled the coffers of political action committees, and brought shining stars down from corporate headquarters (and from Main Street) to testify, confer, and influence. Moreover, the business representatives applied to political organizing the techniques developed for product marketing. They computerized their association membership lists by congressional district and state and utilized the most sophisticated telecommunications equipment to keep in touch with their members.

Although rallying its constituency with elaborate technology has been an important aspect of the business community's strategy, probably more important has been employer organizations' demonstrated willingness to work together. This coalition-building, which necessarily involves subordinating pet ideas to the greater common good, has been a major constraint upon lobbying by employer organizations since company representatives have been careful not to squander political capital on broad issues which have no direct bearing upon their firms' interest.

Business lobbyists have recognized that they lost out in the past by coming to legislators with diverse agendas and legislative wish lists. Now they try to hammer out their priorities before marching up the Hill or attempting to influence the federal bureaucracies. Putting together a "coalition," an "action committee," or an "issue strategy group" is now the first step for the business lobbyist interested in pushing a business organization's legislative priorities. "Solidarity forever" never rang truer.

Joint actions in the political marketplace can further the goal of profit maximization. For example, production costs are vastly affected by occupational health and safety legislation, environmental laws, and labor legislation, whereas prices that producers charge can be influenced by government policies that bolster demand or reduce foreign competition. Beyond the traditional models, profit maximization also entails business actions in the social welfare and political spheres. A century ago, William H. Vanderbilt might have declared "the public be damned," but the modern business community has become concerned about and has tried to cultivate the general public.

Two major forces moved employer factions to put aside rivalries and work together. The first derived from a qualitative change in the nature of federal regulation. As long as federal regulation tended to be industry specific, companies and trade associations had little reason to build political alliances across industrial lines. However, the past twenty years have seen an increase in legislation that has put similar constraints on all industries. Far-reaching laws affecting occupational safety and health, environmental pollution, consumer protection, energy use, and employment discrimination spurred companies in different industries to build legislative coalitions.[3]

Second, the recent dispersion of congressional power has induced lobbyists to work in concert in order to reach their legislative objectives. The breakdown in the seniority system, the subsequent dispersal of power to rank and file members working through subcommittees, and the growth of congressional staffs resulted in the diffusion of power centers on Capitol Hill and the need to win over more people to one's position.[4] With the resultant proliferation of lobbyists in Washington, it became increasingly important for business interests to join forces to cover as many bases as possible, and to win broader support it became necessary to show that a favored law, amendment or regulation would help or harm more than an isolated "special interest." It helped if the lobbyist could show that the entire employer community or a broad cross-section of groups was supporting the desired legislation or the change in regulations.

The three case studies in Part II of this volume illustrate the importance of coordinated employer action in achieving legislative success, and the costs of failure to forge a united front.

In the case of unemployment insurance, employers recognized the potential cost very early and organized pragmatically to keep the program as lean as possible. The employer lobby also succeeded in applying the principles of the new federalism, long before it became a slogan, by limiting the federal government's role and thus leaving much of the program's control in the hands of more sympathetic state legislators. In the fight over pension reform legislation that culminated in the passage of the Employee Retirement Income Security Act (ERISA) in 1974, the business community was slow to recognize a threat and to band together in order to defeat it. Subsequent events have shown the major employer organizations to be more on top of legislative developments in pension policy but still unable to recoup their 1974 losses. The battles over common situs picketing under the Ford administration and labor law reform under the Carter administration demonstrated the return of coalition-building by the business lobbies.

Employer organizations have improved their organizing techniques, not just for defense against federal intrusions but also for offensive actions, particularly now that a politically congenial climate has come to Washington. One key to the improved effectiveness of the business lobbies in recent years has been their pragmatism. Even when employer representatives have viewed a particular welfare program as objectionable, they have understood that its elimination might be anathema to the general public. Rhetoric denouncing a pending bill as "socialist" or "endangering the foundation of freedom" has given way to "attacks on abuses" or "trimming fat" and, above all, emphasis on apparent or potential costs. Frequently, trimming a program can gut it completely, leaving but a shell; of course, this may not be unforeseen by the proponents of cutting back. This is clearly preferable to repeal for it prevents the institution of a much more costly program when the pendulum swings back.

Another lesson learned by Washington business representatives has been the importance of emphasizing the public interest aspects of their position. Of course, it helps that the ideology business has been propounding for years has come into vogue. The once-suspect pronouncement that the "business of America is business" has gained a new respectability and broad support as the portrait of Coolidge has replaced that of Jefferson in the White House. It has been relatively easy, with the shift in political sentiment, to argue that the welfare state has gone too far and is now threatening the free enterprise system. According to this position, the interest in limiting federal regulation is pervasive. We are all in one boat; even if business is the first to benefit from a given rollback or new piece of legislation, the change will eventually help everyone advance to the promised land.

Even a cursory analysis of the business community's new-found élan illustrates that business's strategy and planning have become much more sophisticated and successful. However, the recent successes of business organizations at the national level do not guarantee sustained victory in the future. The business community faces a number of hazards.

First, business is currently playing with close to full deck. The traditional opposition was in disarray in 1981, smarting from the defeats of the 1980 elections and some of the Reagan administration's initial smash successes on Capitol Hill. The liberal-labor coalitions are beginning to reorganize and will undoubtedly stage a comeback. Just as did the business community, the other side has learned from its mistakes and has benefited by observing the activities of its opposition, as evidenced by the 1982 congressional elections. In the political marketplace, it is hard to keep trade secrets.

Second, although the business community seems to have mastered the art of pooling resources and has recognized its short-run advantages, coalition-building also has some potential costs that may be evident only further down the road. Putting together alliances that span the differences within the business community often entails satisfying special interests with tradeoffs and concessions that can undermine the integrity of the coalition's goals.

Special tax benefits, subsidies, or regulatory exemptions can subsequently bring the proposed legislation into question, and if this happens the original coalition may disintegrate. The united front that business lobbies presented in obtaining the tax cuts in 1981 fell apart a year later when the same groups were divided on the merits of a tax increase. Coalitions among employer organizations tend to be rather fragile. The diversity of interests among the parties involved often gives rise to conflicts that prove hard to suppress in the long run.

Third, even powerful coalitions that start out with great advantages can have their momentum broken if they make tactical mistakes and stray too far from the existing political center. The business community's current predominance in the Washington scene may be jeopardized by the early alliances it formed with New Right groups whose interests focused on ideological convictions rather than realistic positions. The alliances that the business lobbyists forged may prove to be neither lasting nor good business.

Finally, there remains the crucial question whether American enterprise "unleashed" from the constraints of government regulation will bring home the bacon. Business has long argued that excessive government regulation and intervention and the lack of proper incentives are largely responsible for current economic and social problems including slow growth, small productivity increases, unemployment problems, inadequate levels of savings and investment, and international trade problems, not to mention the rise in crime and presumed breakdown of the work ethic and the family. Conservatives have laid all these negative developments, real or exaggerated, at the door of liberals—the "big spenders." If the remedies advocated by business do not produce results, then it could be harder to gain acceptance for business's legislative priorities in the future. In a sense, the business community may be vulnerable to attacks similar to those faced by the liberal-labor-minority coalitions. The latter groups promised much more than they could ever hope to deliver, and raised the expectations of their own supporters and the general public. Despite real progress, the results were often measured against inflated promises and found wanting.

It could be that business lobbyists will master these potential problems, but the difficulties cannot be ignored. Although nothing succeeds like success, success also entails having to face up to growing internal conflicts as time passes.

Image

The enhanced effectiveness of employer associations in recent years has coincided with their altered image. The early business associations, while praising rugged individualism, conspired to reduce competition. As T. S. Ashton, a leading historian of the industrial revolution, noted:

> In the eighteenth century the characteristic instrument of social purpose was not the individual or the State, but the club. . . . Many an innocent-looking social or scientific group was, it seems likely, a business organization, the real purpose of which was to blunt the edge of competition and regulate output, prices, wages, or the terms of credit.[5]

Adam Smith, as noted, took a dim view of fraternizing among competitors, a view echoed by America's founding fathers in *The Federalist Papers*. James Madison warned of the "mischief of factions." He was concerned that pressure groups would place their narrow interests above the welfare of the majority. Domestic manufacturers were cited as prime candidates for this potential abuse of power. The hope was that one faction might work to balance out a second group. Yet Madison was not too optimistic: "It is vain to say that enlightened statesmen will be able to adjust these clashing interests and render them all subservient to the public good. Enlightened statesmen will not always be at the helm."[6]

In addition to the concerns voiced by thoughtful social critics, a major constraint on the activities of informal business associations was their poor public relations profile.[7] As a reaction to the robber barons' excesses, a reform movement in the late 1880s and during the first two decades of this century attempted to correct some of the worst abuses wrought by the emerging high corporate concentration. To counteract some major defeats at the hands of reformers, the business community established several new formal employer associations in the place of earlier informal institutions. These business associations were soon able to blunt reform drives by effecting either repeal of legislation or weakening of enforcement. A prime example of this process was the formation of the Interstate Commerce Commission in 1887 to regulate railroads. Under business pressure, the ICC remained weak. Similarly, state laws passed on fair labor standards were ineffective and often unenforced.[8]

By the middle of this century social scientists had put forward theories to justify and explain the workings of special interest groups, including employers' organizations. Government was nothing more than the battleground of conflicting groups, and each interested party had to seek its own advocate either in the form of an association or private representative.[9] David B. Truman

painted business groups as an integral part of government in action. He credited
these associations with a major role in obtaining access to policymakers and
helping political leaders come into contact with influential segments of the
business community.[10] Extending the paradigm of the marketplace for goods
and services, economists have tried to demonstrate the workings of a political
marketplace. Instead of dollars and cents, the legal tender in this marketplace is
votes and influence. Pressure groups were shown to play a vital role in the
optimal workings of this political marketplace; without them, full expression of
major interests' views would be impossible and the common good would not be
satisfactorily articulated.[11] A leading business executive argued:

> "We businessmen have . . . heedlessly neglected to pay enough
> attention to politics and politicians. We have thus failed even to
> recognize, much less equip ourselves to meet, new and unfamiliar
> managerial requirements in connection with political problems of such
> constantly mounting importance."[12]

This positive role for special interest groups has been questioned recently
because their effectiveness depends so much upon their resources. Wealthy
segments of society find it far easier to form pressure groups, further tightening
their hold on society. Some analysts of the pressure group process have questioned whether the government has lost its ability to stand up to these coalitions,
and others have asserted that the government, pressured by narrow private
forces, has abdicated its social responsibilities.[13]

For Better or Worse

Business has been wide open to charges of power abuse in the political
spectrum and in the marketplace. The illegal corporate campaign contributions
in the 1972 presidential election and some labor political activities raised public
concern about undue business and union influence in national elections, and led
business and labor to support the 1974 and 1976 amendments to the campaign
financing laws.[14] However, the solutions offered by these reforms turned out to
be more serious than the problems. The new law stimulated the expansion of
political action committees (PACs), which have been able to circumvent the
earlier limits on contributions.

The heightened visibility of business in Washington and its increased success
rate on Capitol Hill will very likely give rise to increased concern about the
political role of employers' organizations. This will be particularly true if the
public perceives that the favors business has received in Washington do not lead
to marketplace improvements such as economic growth and the creation of jobs
providing equal opportunity to women and minorities.

The debate over the proper role of pressure groups—business as well as labor and other social coalitions—is as old as the republic. There is every reason to expect that this debate will continue into the future. Where once it was argued with quill pens and printing presses, the debate is now carried on with computer printouts and electronic messages, but the substance of the arguments and the cast of protagonists have changed little. The influence of these formal and informal associations remains crucial to understanding the direction of social policies and economic results. For better or worse, it is difficult to picture our mixed economy without such strong associations.

2

The Old
Establishment

It is not big business that we have to fear.
It is big government.
—Wendell L. Wilkie

Many Mansions

Wilkie's warning might have served as a rallying cry for the organization of business lobbies. By the end of the nineteenth century business leaders perceived that the highly informal specialized business clubs of the 1800s were inadequate to meet the challenges of the national progressive and labor movements. A first generation of formal business organizations was created to counter these reform drives. The Great Depression and the New Deal raised new concerns and challenges to employers, and a new generation of business associations was formed. In the 1970s the business community felt it needed new institutions to counter drives by liberal, labor, and minority coalitions, and this resulted in still more formal business groups.

Although the business community in the United States has made notable advances in presenting its views to government policymakers and to the public, no single dominant organization exists, as it does in several European countries, to speak for business on major national policy issues. Nor are there even two organizations, as in the Federal Republic of Germany, one to speak on economic questions and the other to deal with social issues. The number and diversity of these organizations in America reflect the size and pluralism of our economy. Most prominent of these all-industry organizations are the National Association of Manufacturers, the Chamber of Commerce of the United States, the Business Roundtable, and the American Business Conference, the latest arrival on the scene.

In addition, there are the Committee for Economic Development and the Business Council, organizations that do not formally engage in lobbying. The Committee, composed of business executives assisted by academics, explores a variety of policy questions and issues periodic policy statements. The Council provides a forum for informal exchanges of views between top business and government executives but does not take formal positions as an organization. Small business is represented by a number of organizations, the largest being the National Federation of Independent Business. These organizations, representing employers from a range of economic sectors, often ally themselves with trade and industry associations in pursuit of specific legislative goals.

National Association of Manufacturers

The National Association of Manufacturers is the senior national business organization. With a current membership of some 13,500 manufacturing firms, it claims to be the "voice of American industry." Although its membership accounts for only 3 percent of manufacturing enterprises in the United States, the members of the Association account for 75 percent of the nation's industrial output and provide about the same percentage of its industrial employment. The NAM also claims to speak on occasion for the 160,000 companies that belong to the 260 independent state manufacturing and business associations, national trade groups, and industrial relations organizations.

The NAM was founded in 1894 in response to the urging of the editor of *The Dixie Manufacturer* to establish an organization to promote foreign trade, but a major coal strike soon shifted the new association's primary interest to industrial relations. The organization's *Declaration of Principles* in 1903 established the NAM as an opponent of unionism and a proponent of the so-called open shop, a stance which colored its activities for several decades. Although the NAM's position on labor and social issues has mellowed over time, industrial relations has remained one of its principal areas of concern.

From its start, the NAM was made up largely of small manufacturers. But the vehement opposition of many business leaders to the New Deal required a platform from which to attack the new social reforms. The NAM provided the needed forum.

The NAM campaign against Roosevelt's reforms galvanized the business community and yielded large increases in both membership and income. Since the 1930s, there have been repeated shifts in the proportions of smaller and larger firms on the NAM board of directors, although owners or officials of small and medium-sized businesses remain the backbone of the organization.[1] In 1981, 44 percent of its member firms employed fewer than 100 people, 63 percent had fewer than 200 employees, and 80 percent employed fewer than 500 people. Nevertheless, about two-fifths of the more than 200 NAM board members were employed by firms on the Fortune 500 list, indicating a heavy representation of big business in the organization's leadership. Such men are of course desirable for their prominence, but the reason for their relatively large representation on the board may be that a few large corporations provide a disproportionate part of the NAM's income. Membership dues are calculated on a sliding scale geared to the net worth of companies, and virtually all of the organization's expenses are met through dues. A number of corporations, such as General Motors, DuPont, and General Electric, make yearly contributions of $75,000; the minimum fee for companies with a net worth of under $300,000 is $100. In 1981, the NAM's budget was approximately $10 million.

The NAM currently has fourteen policy committees, ranging in size from 50 to 400 members, with an aggregate membership of 2500. The areas covered by these committees include international economic affairs, resources and technology, taxation and fiscal policy, government regulation and competition, and industrial relations. The five units that constitute the industrial relations committee are concerned with labor relations, human resources and equal opportunity, employee benefits, occupational safety and health, and compensation systems.

Member participation centers on policy formulation, which is ironed out in the committees. They are headed by members chosen by the board, and some of the larger committees have smaller steering groups. As is normal in voluntary organizations, committee chairmen and NAM staff members tend to dominate policy formulation. Since the interests and views represented by the members are frequently diverse, the staff-prepared resolutions attempt as a rule to present a consensus, thus avoiding clashes among the members. This accounts for the richness of rhetoric and paucity of solid analysis in many NAM policy statements. The board of directors has final say on policy proposals made by the committees, but substantial changes in committee policy recommendations are rare.

In 1982, the NAM employed 205 staff members, of whom approximately 120 were based in Washington. The bulk of the staff effort is devoted to servicing the policy committees, monitoring legislative, regulatory, and judicial developments, and presenting the NAM viewpoint to policymakers and the public. Before the NAM's move to Washington in 1974, its profile in the capital was much lower than today, as the small Washington staff did very little day-to-day lobbying on the Hill. Its main job was monitoring legislative developments, though it also did some "firefighting" on legislation that it viewed as antibusiness.

The main reason for the move to Washington was to give the NAM greater clout there. In December 1972, Burt F. Raynes, then NAM Chairman, explained:

> We had been in New York since before the turn of the century, because we regarded this city as the center of business and industry. But the thing that affects business most today is government. The inter-relationship of business with business is no longer so important as the inter-relationship of business with government. In the last several years, that has become very apparent to us.[2]

The move was also intended to facilitate closer cooperation with the Chamber of Commerce of the United States and to make the NAM more visible to the press.

Indicative of the NAM's relatively recent emphasis on influencing federal policy was its decision in 1975 to register with Congress as an organization whose principal activity is lobbying. Individual NAM employees had registered previously as lobbyists, but the organization had insisted that lobbying was not its main activity. The NAM explained that its 1975 decision reflected not a change in its attitude toward the law but a shift of the group's emphasis. A suit filed against the NAM by Common Cause the previous year probably also influenced NAM's formal acknowledgment of its primary function. In 1982, the NAM staff included more than twenty full-time, registered lobbyists.

Even before the NAM moved to Washington, it attempted to reverse its public image as a naysayer to all government social welfare interventions and to create a more positive image. The efforts included a manpower training project for minorities, an industry alternative to truth-in-packaging laws, and a project designed to let NAM members exchange information on ways of dealing with employee problems.

In the 1980s, emphasis has been placed on providing service functions for industry, especially for small manufacturers who do not have the resources to hire their own representation in Washington. One particularly popular innovation has been NAM teleconferences that explain various federal programs, such as safety and health regulations, to members.

The NAM's focus on new public policy developments has not displaced its traditional management concerns. Responding to pressures from small non-union employers, it established in December 1977 the Council for Union-free Environment (CUE) to sponsor research and seminars and to act as a clearinghouse for information on employee relations programs that enable employers to avoid union organization. Though CUE's membership spans the spectrum of company size, representatives from small firms predominate, and four of every five CUE members are NAM members as well. CUE has its own membership and fee structure, and a budget that amounted to $300,000 in

1982, financed by its 525 members. Although CUE has remained a NAM affiliate, it has never received full-fledged recognition in the association. By the end of 1982, it was the sole subsidiary in the association without the privilege of proposing legislation; although still a member of the family, some would prefer to deny its legitimacy. Whatever the status of CUE within the NAM, the AFL-CIO saw the formation of CUE as an attempt of the NAM to revive an attack on unionization.

The NAM also maintains a substantial program of grass-roots education and political mobilization through various journals and newsletters. It does not have its own political action committee, though it was instrumental in the founding of the Business and Industry Political Action Committee in 1963. Instead, it publishes the *PAC Manager,* a monthly newsletter that advises members on how to set up and manage PACs and occasionally analyzes issues in national races in which there is member interest.

Evaluations of NAM's ability to represent its members to the federal government have invariably concluded that the organization tends to preach to the converted. The association's desire to become the dominant voice for industry in government-business dealings has been constantly thwarted by the presence in Washington of the Chamber of Commerce, which in 1981 represented more than twice as many manufacturers as the NAM.

The NAM has traditionally been viewed as the more conservative of the two national business organizations, particularly on social welfare and labor issues, though this is much less true today. The reduction of taxes and government controls has always been high on the NAM's agenda, but these issues have not generally been accorded the same order of importance as the longstanding battle with organized labor. The NAM no longer claims that social security will lead to "ultimate socialistic control of life and industry."[3] In recent years, under the leadership of Alexander Trowbridge, Secretary of Commerce during the Johnson administration, NAM has adopted a more open-minded, flexible style.

In the past, NAM's tendency to adopt relatively extreme positions on national policy issues has hindered its ability to influence policy. In fact, as a result of its poor legislative track record, the NAM's approval of specific legislation was characterized some three decades ago as the "kiss of death."[4] The NAM's lack of credibility among legislators, declining membership, and insufficient finances put pressure on the Association to change its approach. Membership peaked in 1957 at 22,000 companies and has gradually declined since then, yet progressive fee increases made NAM's income in 1981 the highest ever. The organizational face-lifts began with the appointment in 1962 of W. P. Gullander, the first full-time president of NAM. He prided himself on being "a conservative who wants to face up to the future" and did a great deal to open up channels of communication with the federal government—even with the National Labor Relations Board, long considered the NAM's whipping boy. Gullander also instituted the "problem-solving approach," by which the NAM was to present workable alternatives to legislation that it opposed.[5]

The NAM has continued to grapple with the joint problems of arresting the decline in its membership and developing an identity separate from that of the Chamber. It has tried to focus on issues of specific interest to manufacturers and to avoid spreading its resources too thin. Alexander Trowbridge, who took over as president in 1980, has continued the efforts of his predecessors to rework the NAM's obstructionist image and to develop more constructive approaches to legislative issues. To allow the staff elbow room in their lobbying activities, the NAM has attempted to adopt flexible policy resolutions. The association's position on social security illustrates the application of the flexible approach favored by Trowbridge. In the fall of 1982, when amendments to social security legislation were pending before Congress, the NAM abandoned its earlier policy, which preached fiscal responsibility and a stable dollar, and suggested instead a series of options that would assure the solvency of the social security system. In releasing its revised policy statement the NAM board of directors claimed that the new policy was merely a "clarification and expansion of existing NAM opinion,"[6] but the spelling out of options brought the NAM policy into the mainstream of debate on this vital subject and gave the staff a blueprint for action rather than limiting them to defending pious pronouncements.

Trowbridge has made overtures to organized labor, but the unions are understandably suspicious of the hand being extended. In particular, their reservations center on the existence of the Council for Union-Free Environment, which they consider a union-busting organization—a present-day version of the NAM's past open shop advocacy. Nevertheless, as *the Wall Street Journal* has noted: "Trowbridge is trying to bring NAM into the twentieth century."[7]

Chamber of Commerce of the United States

The Chamber of Commerce of the United States, an organization that the NAM helped to found in 1912, has long since established itself as the preeminent voice for American business—to the apparent detraction of its parent. The Chamber originated in a period that saw the birth of numerous trade and civic organizations. Businessmen at that time perceived threats both from labor and from the government's antitrust efforts and also saw the potential for expansion of international trade. With the multiplicity of business organizations, there was a need for "an association of associations," and this need was not met by the NAM or any other business organization.[8]

It is ironic that a number of local chambers of commerce enlisted the help of the federal government in creating the national Chamber when their independent efforts failed. In 1912, at the instruction of President William Taft, his secretary of labor and commerce convened a conference of commercial associations in Washington and called for the creation of a centralized organization that could speak for business on national issues. .Twenty-four associations out of the 234 represented at that conference formed the Chamber of Commerce of the United States.

The Chamber is now a federation of 257,000 business and organization members. The business members—mostly firms, with some individual business people—constitute the vast majority of the membership. The organizational members are trade and professional associations and local, state, and regional chambers of commerce. Unlike the NAM, the Chamber's membership has grown steadily in boom times and recessions (with the exception of the period 1931–33); membership has more than quadrupled since 1976. The biggest gain occurred between April 1981 and mid-1982, when the membership surpassed 250,000, reflecting in part the close association of the Chamber with the Reagan administration. The Chamber capitalized on the association and an intensified membership drive paid off. Companies with less than ten employees accounted for 70 percent of the increase during the Reagan administration.

The Chamber draws its members from all segments of the business community, including agricultural employers, manufacturers, and doctors and dentists (the latter are classed under ''services'') (table 1). The Chamber represents businesses from a broader range of sectors than the NAM, and counts among its members many small and medium-sized businesses as well.

The general orientation of Chamber policy, however, tends to reflect big business concerns rather than those of small business. Just as in the NAM, this is in part because big business provides a share of the Chamber's income out of proportion to its members. The minimum annual membership dues in 1982 were $125, but some companies pay much more. There is no single dues schedule for Chamber membership.

The big business orientation in Chamber policy also reflects the preponderance of executives from large corporations on the Chamber's board of directors. Of sixty-four directors in 1981, twenty-four were executives of corporations on the Fortune 500 list for that year, accounting for 38 percent of the Chamber's board, as compared with 42 percent of the NAM board members who were from companies on the same list. Big business's domination of the Chamber's board is even more striking than in the case of the NAM because the average size of a member firm in the Chamber is much smaller than that of an NAM member; only 22.7 percent of the NAM's members employ fewer than fifty employees, compared with 87 percent of the Chamber's business members.

Table 1
Chamber of Commerce Business Membership, April 1981

	Membership	Percentage of Total Membership	Number of Establishments
Total	119,600	100.0	4,536,000
Manufacturing	26,600	22.2	321,000
Services	19,900	16.6	1,262,000
Retail	22,600	18.9	1,237,000
Wholesale	13,100	11.0	383,000
Construction	14,000	11.7	447,000
Finance, insurance, real estate	11,900	9.9	425,000
Transportation, communication, utilities	5,200	4.3	168,000
Agricultural services, mining	6,300	5.3	74,000

Source: Let's Rebuild America: 1981 Annual Report, Chamber of Commerce of the United States, p. 30; and *Statistical Abstracts of the United States*, 1981, p. 536.

Note: In addition to these business members, the Chamber has as organizational members approximately 2,800 state, local, and regional chambers of commerce, 44 American chambers abroad, and about 1,400 trade and professional associations. Total includes nonclassifiable establishments not shown separately.

In an effort to modify its image as a "big business lobby," and to increase small business input to the policymaking process, the Chamber established in 1976 a separate center for small business with an advisory group to focus exclusively on small business concerns.

In 1982, the Chamber had approximately thirty committees, task forces, and panels involving upwards of 1300 business, professional, and educational representatives, some of whom were not members of the Chamber. The Chamber's policy concerns are broader than those of the NAM. This is understandable given the rather greater resources the Chamber has at its disposal. The Chamber's 1982 budget was over $80 million, almost nine times larger than that of the NAM. Policy committees are officially appointed by the Chamber president and are reconstituted annually. Recommendations for committee appointments are made by the Chamber's policy staff with the aid of local chamber executives and interested corporate officials and are rarely questioned by the president. Committee chairmen are usually members of the Chamber's board of directors and are generally CEOs or board chairmen; committee members tend to be lower-level executives.

Because membership of the policy committees changes so frequently, Chamber staff generally exert a great deal of influence over the policymaking process. The Chamber employs about 1400 people at its Washington head-quarters and about 600 people in the field. Not only are staff members involved in the membership selection process, but they also provide the bulk of the committees' information and are chiefly responsible for the implementation of policy as well. Through careful staff maneuvering, the committees often come to reflect the viewpoint of the committee staff. Thus, over the years, committees have come to represent certain predictable positions on policy. It is this pervasive influence of the staff that led the late Chamber chief economist, Carl Madden, to compare the organization's operations with those of most large corporations. He noted ''a general tendency in the Chamber, similar to that in many corporations, by which the staff assumes control over the 'owners.' ''[9]

But conflicts erupt even in the most smoothly run institutions. In August 1982, President Reagan pushed for a tax increase to reduce the anticipated deficit caused by the huge cuts of the previous year. Chamber president Richard Lesher remained true to supply side economics and opposed the tax boost even though the federal budget was facing a deficit estimated at $100 to $130 billion, depending upon who was doing the guessing (the actual deficit was $100.7 billion). But Paul Thayer, chairman of the Chamber board and CEO of LTV Corporation, and thirty of the sixty-one Chamber board members (there were four vacancies) supported President Reagan. Relying on the Chamber constitution, which requires a two-thirds vote to change policy, Lesher stuck to his guns and publicly opposed the tax cut. The rift was publicized, and according to one report the freewheeling of the staff was to be curtailed—Thayer expected the board to establish ''a very clear understanding as to what the relationship is between the Chamber and the board.''[10]

Thayer apparently won this confrontation. The Chamber board approved a resolution stating that it ''should be given the opportunity to consider significant acts or matters of potential controversy involving the implementation of interpretation of policy.''[11] The catch, however, was that the board adopted its resolution on November 9, 1982, one week after the election and after Congress approved the tax cut favored by President Reagan. One month later President Reagan nominated Thayer for the number two spot in the Defense Department. Thayer of course relinquished his post with the Chamber, which would have expired in 1983; Lesher, aged forty-nine in 1982, is likely to remain at the helm for many more years.

In the 1970s, the Chamber engaged in an extensive public relations campaign. The campaign originated with a memorandum written by Justice Lewis F. Powell in August 1971, just before he was nominated to the Supreme Court. This memo analyzed the reasons for business's poor public image and outlined a multifaceted strategy to remedy the situation. In addition to an active media campaign and stepped-up political activity, Powell recommended making the Chamber presidency a full-time permanent post rather than an elective honorary position, courting more friends in the academic community, and undertaking more extensive litigation than had been previously attempted. All of these recommendations have been implemented.

The most concrete expression of Justice Powell's strategy has been the establishment in 1977 of the National Chamber Litigation Center. The NCLC is a business-oriented public interest law firm whose purpose is to promote the private enterprise viewpoint before the courts and regulatory agencies. The center was formed in reaction both to the proliferation of lawsuits filed by "antibusiness" groups since the 1960s and to the growth of "judicial activism," under which the courts have been interpreting the law rather more broadly—and liberally—than business would like.[12]

The NCLC litigation strategy has given the Chamber a much greater visibility than it had before. The center has concentrated thus far on occupational safety and health, environmental, and pension plan regulations. The main criterion for taking a case is that it have a potential impact on a broad cross-section of the business community. In addition to litigation, the center also undertakes some legal research. Its activities are supported by contributions from companies, associations, and individuals, and the Chamber itself defrays some overhead expenses. The center is governed by a seven-member board of directors, all of whom are also on the Chamber board.

Because the Chamber's primary function is to influence Congress, most commentators have taken its lobbying performance as a general measure of its effectiveness. It is difficult to evaluate lobbying effectiveness, but it is clear that the Chamber's impact has been enhanced during the 1970s by membership participation in the lobbying and legislative process. The Chamber's extensive grass-roots organization has come to be its primary means of influence; direct lobbying of legislators by Chamber staff is of secondary importance in the Chamber's strategy.

The backbone of the Chamber's grass-roots operation is some 2,700 congressional action committees (CACs) (although many of these local units are inactive). First established in 1951 through the efforts of local and state chambers of commerce, member corporations began to form independent CACs only in 1975. Direct lobbying is frequently complemented by testimony before congressional committees. The frequency of testimony by CACs does not change the fact that their positions on issues are viewed by members of Congress and their staffs as being fairly predictable. The Chamber is given relatively high marks for its visibility and its ability to get its points across, if not always for its ability to persuade.

Unlike the NAM, the Chamber has not registered under the 1946 lobby act because it maintains that direct lobbying is not its principal organizational activity. However, many of its eighty-five issue managers and fifteen legislative staffers are registered as lobbyists. Issue managers are responsible for following legislation through Congress, coordinating Chamber strategy, and briefing the membership about the issues. On important issues, Chamber members will be brought in to present the testimony. In 1981, Chamber representatives testified ninety-four times before congressional committees.

The Chamber's reliance on prepared materials and formal testimony reflects the limitations of its federated structure when it comes to the day-to-day maneuvering over technical but frequently significant changes in the language of a bill. In 1972, the White House official for congressional relations commented: "The problem with a conglomerate lobby like the Chamber is that they are not equipped to make day-to-day decisions to make an impact. Any major policy decision requires a board meeting."[13] This lack of flexibility has not changed, as noted in the case of the 1982 tax boosts. On the other hand, the Chamber's structure gives it an advantage in rallying grass-roots support.

Because of the Chamber's size, finances, research and communications facilities, and the geographical dispersion of its membership, it is an ideal ally for single-issue groups looking to form coalitions. Moreover, the Chamber itself realizes that the success of its campaigns for specific bills depends upon coordination with other like-minded organizations. To cultivate its relations with other business lobbies, the Chamber hosts biweekly breakfasts for corporate representatives and staff members of the Washington-based trade and professional associations. Top Chamber officials also meet regularly with NAM executives. Moreover, Chamber staff members participate in the activities of other groups that share the Chamber's views on a wide range of issues.

Until recently, the Chamber's efforts have been concentrated on Congress, and relatively little time has been spent trying to influence policymaking at the White House. This has been true under both Democratic and Republican administrations. When the White House has needed to hear the "business viewpoint" on policy, it has tended to call in individual members of the Business Roundtable, Business Council, or Committee for Economic Development because of their personal reputations as business leaders, not because of their membership in the Chamber. This has changed rather strikingly under the Reagan administration, which shares the ideology of an organization that prides itself on being the "keeper of the faith" in the business community. Also, the Reagan White House aides do not need "instruction on the workings of the market or the costs of regulation. What they need is help in putting grass roots pressure on Democratic congressmen—something the Roundtable's executive-suite celebrities are ill-equipped to do."[14] The Chamber's grass-roots organization is presumably well suited to the task. This view is not universally held, however. Roundtable boosters suggest that their organization may in many instances be more effective than the Chamber because the members of the Roundtable operate branch offices or plants in virtually every congressional district and they can mobilize the managers of the subordinate units for action, whereas the Chamber must depend upon its staff members to stir up the troops at the local level.

In 1982, the Chamber launched an ambitious satellite television program that President Reagan thought could potentially "promote and strengthen our enterprise system." This American Business Network (BizNet) was to serve as a nationwide business communication system. As envisoned by the Chamber, BizNet would not only provide news and commentary on matters of interest to business, but would also stress lobbying and political activities. Although they don't proclaim so for the record, Chamber staff members predict that through BizNet the organization will be the dominant voice of business. The *Nation's Business* approved presidential counsellor Edwin Meese's prediction that BizNet will "revolutionize the way the business community makes itself heard."[15] But at least one Chamber staff member expressed the concern that the BizNet may turn out to be "Lesher's folly." One political commentator observed:

> It is too early to have the vaguest idea of whether this latest com-
> munications revolution will prove to be much of a revolution at all.
> But it is certain to be good business and a capital new way for players
> to trade and maintain power in the great American campaign game.
> The ideologues will try to sell their messages, technicians seek to
> prove the efficacy of their machines and managers run about hysteri-
> cally in pursuit of the next sweet political deal, all in about the same
> proportion as they have operated since shortly after the beginning of
> the republic.[16]

Attempted Merger
and Persisting Differences

During the 1970s, some NAM and Chamber leaders made an effort to merge the two organizations. The initial steps were taken by the senior organization. Upon assuming the presidency of the NAM in 1973, E. Douglas Kenna initiated efforts to coordinate NAM activities with other business organ-
izations, notably the Chamber. He and Chamber Executive Vice President Arch N. Booth held biweekly summit conferences designed to eliminate the antagonism stemming from their competition for members and for recognition as the leading voice of business. The two organizations cosponsored a number of conferences, conducted some joint research, and took joint positions on a few issues. In October 1972, the NAM and the Chamber wrote their first joint letter urging President Nixon to promptly remove all wage and price controls. A

year later the two organizations established a joint committee to counter what the business community perceived as antibusiness public sentiment and the political threat that this posed.

There has been talk of merging the Chamber and the NAM ever since the former was founded in 1912. However, discussions advanced in the mid-1970s for several reasons. First, the business community felt then that with increasing government regulation and the public acceptance of governmental intervention, the interests and prerogatives of the business community were in serious jeopardy. As James Sites, former senior vice president for communications at the NAM, put it: "The business community feels threatened as never before. It's a feeling of public misunderstanding, of hostility, even of belligerence."[17] In short, it was time to circle the wagons.

Second, by the mid-1970s there were relatively few philosophical differences separating the Chamber and the NAM. The NAM was still more conservative and generally represented larger companies than the Chamber, but the organizations agreed on most issues and felt that they could reconcile whatever differences remained.

Third, Richard Lesher had taken over the leadership of the Chamber in 1975. This change of leadership was the first in twenty-five years. Lesher's predecessor, Arch Booth, had built up the Chamber, but the organization had lost momentum towards the end of Booth's tenure. Until Booth was prepared to step down, many business leaders who viewed a NAM-Chamber merger as desirable were not inclined to push for it.

Fourth, the NAM's move to Washington, intended to give the organization a stronger voice as the representative of business, actually served to reduce its effectiveness because there it was thwarted by the Chamber. The NAM had served a constituency of corporate officers when it was in New York. Once in Washington, it weakened the ties with its old constituency and was unable to compete with the well-entrenched Chamber in the new location.

For these reasons, observers were more likely to view the merger as a "marriage of convenience" than to accept the parties' version that it was a long romance that was late in blooming.[18] The merged organization was intended to strengthen the political clout of organized business in Washington much as the 1955 merger of the AFL and the CIO had increased the political clout of organized labor. The merger was also intended to reduce the duplication of services provided by the two organizations, and to consolidate resources and expand research facilities in order to be able to deal with more policy issues in greater depth. Although information on duplicate membership in both organizations is not available, the overlap has been considerable. At the time the merger was being considered, the Chamber had a membership of 56,000 business firms and 3,500 organizations and annual revenue of approximately $13 million, compared with the NAM's 13,000 corporate members and annual income of $7 million.

Combining in true Solomonic fashion the names of both organizations, the merged establishment was to be known as the Association of Commerce and Industry. It was to have been headed by Lesher and based in the Chamber's headquarters across Lafayette Park from the White House. NAM President Kenna was to head a council comprising top officials of each organization to set policy during the transition period. The executive boards of both organizations approved the merger in principle in June of 1976 and it was expected to go through smoothly. In September, however, the NAM board unanimously rejected the merger proposal and called instead for a "joint council" to coordinate the activities of the two separate organizations and minimize duplication. The joint council has met periodically since that time.

A number of problems stood in the way of the planned merger. Possibly foremost was the apprehension on the part of many NAM leaders that industry's voice would be muted in the new organization because of the preponderance of nonmanufacturing companies among the Chamber's members. They felt that having a separate organization guaranteed the rigorous presentation of the interests of manufacturers, whose needs differ from those of other business sectors. Second, small businesses in both organizations feared domination by big business interests in the new organization and strongly resisted the merger. Other obstacles were mostly concerned with egos and turf rather than substance. One of these was the fact that the NAM's board had 175 members and the Chamber's only 65. The NAM's demand for 50–50 representation on the consolidated 100-member board created difficulties. Finally, the role of the staffs in both organizations cannot be ignored. Had the merger been approved, staff cuts were a distinct probability and loss of status for some would have been inevitable. The power of the bureaucracies in both organizations should not be underestimated.

Overall, the national Chamber has been considered generally more effective as a national business lobby than the NAM. The advantages of staff size, membership, and federated structure are clear and explain its greater clout. However, under the current leadership of the two organizations, it appears that the Chamber is projecting a more inflexible ideological image than the NAM. Lesher's Chamber has become much more aggressive and ideological, particularly since the 1980 elections, as indicated by the Chamber's unyielding position on the 1982 Reagan tax increase. The NAM supported the President's position, which pure supply side economists considered heresy. The NAM's new image also reflects President Alexander Trowbridge's emphasis on flexibility.

The NAM and the Chamber are distinguished from other national business organizations by their membership, structure, and origins. Their memberships include a large number of small and medium-sized businesses, even though their boards of directors have significant big business representation and their pronouncements are frequently indistinguishable from the views of those organizations representing exclusively big business. In contrast, the Business Council, the Committee for Economic Development, and the Business Roundtable unabashedly represent big business interests, and the National Federation of Independent Business, the National Small Business Association, and the Small Business Legislative Council exclusively represent the "smalls."

The NAM and the Chamber are also distinguished by their being broad-based "mass membership" organizations; the business organizations that followed them offer membership only to select individuals. Consequently, the NAM and the Chamber rely heavily on extensive staff support for most of their activities, and the CED and the Business Roundtable involve to a much greater degree corporate executives in both policy formation and lobbying.

Lastly, the big business organizations are distinguished by their origins. These, in turn, have had an influence on their respective ideological orientations. The NAM and the Chamber date back to the pre–New Deal era when federal intervention in business operations was minimal. In contrast, the Business Council, the Business Roundtable, and the CED were organized to seek business responses to the expanding welfare state. The public pronouncements of the second group of organizations have tended to reflect greater acceptance of the government's role in a mixed economy than those of the first generation of business organizations. Although these ideological differences have narrowed considerably in recent years, they are still evident in that the NAM and the Chamber have their closest political ties with conservative Republicans and southern Democrats, whereas the CED–Business Council–Business Roundtable group has greater influence with the centrist wing of both parties.[19]

3

Employer Associations in a Mixed Economy

I am for the New Deal, then, because I am a business man.
—Edward A. Filene

Peace-making with the Inevitable

Writing in 1934, the nationally prominent merchant Edward A. Filene represented a small minority among his peers, many of whom considered Franklin D. Roosevelt a traitor to his class. But Filene, who was an early organizer of the Chamber of Commerce of the United States, saw things differently. The New Deal was "not a new solution for old problems," he asserted. It was a "solution for a new problem—a problem arising from the evolution of machine industry and the evolution of American society."[1] There was no going back. FDR's goal was to boost aggregate demand and reduce unemployment by increasing production. The early New Deal game plan was embodied in the National Industrial Recovery Act (NRA), which was essentially an attempt to fight the Depression through a system of price and wage codes. It was hoped that the codes would block further deflationary forces.

Despite objections from some business circles, Filene pointed out that business had always operated under a code—whether custom or law. It was only a question of which code it would be. He questioned whether the older code, based on custom, was suitable under highly developed and concentrated economic conditions. The Committee for Economic Development was founded less than a decade after Filene endorsed the New Deal. According to Alfred C. Neal, a former CED president, "the original CED trustees knew that the self-regulating economy was dead, and they were trying to figure out what to put in its place."[2]

Realizing that governmental intervention could help bolster profits and provide economic and social stability, other employers eventually saw some merit in his views. Business interests were in far better shape in the early 1930s to press their advantage than either labor or government. Many of the NRA codes of fair competition, for example, were drafted by business trade associations or industry executives. When industry and labor clashed over the NRA codes, industry won in every case.[3]

As governmental intervention in economic affairs expanded, the business community experienced a love-hate relationship with the new institutions. On the one hand, business executives thought there was something that seemed almost un-American about what the New Dealers were doing; on the other hand, many programs produced major benefits for business.

FDR and succeeding presidents have felt ambivalent toward the business community. Democratic leaders have often tried to cultivate support among business executives, but they have also felt strong antipathy toward them. President Kennedy's administration was typical of this pattern, vacillating between praising business leaders and attacking them. The leaders of many of the nation's larger corporations were Johnson administration supporters, yet later many of these same executives vehemently attacked the Great Society. Republican presidents often have seemed the natural allies of business, but GOP leaders have also had stormy encounters with the captains of industry. President Eisenhower's farewell address was an attack on the military-industrial complex, and President Nixon instituted wage and price controls, which were anathema to business.

The welfare state has provided the business community with both challenges and opportunities. A major goal of employer associations has been to maximize benefits for their constituents and to minimize the costs of governmental intervention that accompany the expansion of social programs. Social welfare programs can help companies substantially by encouraging social stability even during very rough economic periods and by mitigating wrenching economic booms and busts. Unemployment insurance, welfare payments, food stamps, medical care, subsidized housing, and public employment and training programs all take pressure off employers when workers are laid off in a slump or in response to technological change. The benefits are welcomed by business leaders—but not the costs.

The business community has, for the most part, opposed social welfare and labor programs as they have been proposed in Congress; at least initially, all they can see is the cost involved—a stance that comes naturally to American business leaders devoted to free market operations. It is only later, once the programs have been enacted, that the long-run benefits become apparent. As one thoughtful government official noted:

> Who among the business community today would seriously propose that Congress repeal our child labor laws—or the Sherman Anti-Trust Act? The Federal Reserve Act, the Security Exchange Act? Or Workmen's Compensation? Or Social Security? Or Minimum Wage? Or Medicare? Or civil rights legislation? All of us today recognize that such legislation is an integral part of our system; that it has made us a stronger, more prosperous nation—and, in the long run, has been good for business. But we can take precious little credit for any of the social legislation now on the books, for business vigorously opposed most of this legislation—and we get precious little credit from the people.[4]

With the advent of the welfare state and the expansion of governmental intervention, business associations became a major growth industry. Their members attempted to increase organizational strength to counteract governmental encroachment upon their preserves. Particularly pronounced was the employers' clamor to establish a united business front to offset excessive union power, real and supposed. A national survey in 1960 found that farmers, laborers, and white-collar workers believed that business was more powerful than labor, whereas business executives and professionals thought that organized labor had greater influence over Congress than employers.[5]

The growth of the welfare state has forced the business community to pay closer attention to affairs in Washington. Despite the shifting balance of power and variously expressed public sentiments (depending on the political and economic season), the love-hate relationship between the business community and the advocates of a mixed economy continues. The search for the free lunch—or for someone who will pick up the bill—is unending.

The Voice of Business Elites

In contrast to the older business organizations, which have continued to yearn for bygone days, the business groups formed since the New Deal have tended to take governmental intervention for granted and have tried to accommodate their interests to those of the expanding state. Notable among these organizations are the Business Council, Business Roundtable, and the Committee for Economic Development, all of which represent the larger blue-chip corporations. The American Business Conference, the junior business organization of executives from mid-sized corporations, is rapidly growing in influence and may claim to be included in the roster of major business organizations. Unlike the Chamber of Commerce or the NAM, membership in this newer generation of employer associations tends to be on an individual—not company—basis. In fact, membership in these groups indicates elevation to the status of the nation's highest business elite. The membership lists of the Business Council and the Business Roundtable are almost identical; the CED, though less exclusive, shares some of the same members.

The Business Council

The origins of the Business Council coincide with the rise of the welfare state. Established in the same year as the New Deal, it was to provide "the most experienced . . . advice as to proper ways of stimulating and reviving the economy."[6] The idea originated with the late Sidney Weinberg, then a senior partner of the New York investment banking firm of Goldman Sachs, who recognized that business's resistance to the new reforms was doomed to failure. Roosevelt seized the opportunity to have a constructive dialogue with the business community, and the Council was established as a quasi-governmental body within the Department of Commerce. Its original membership included executives of major corporations and a sprinkling of executives from medium-sized companies. It has maintained its blue-chip character ever since.

The Council, as it turned out, had a rather tense relationship with the Roosevelt administration. The only significant area of agreement between them concerned social security, and consultation with the Business Advisory Council—as it was called then—was not as frequent as the business leaders had originally hoped. Though individual members of the Council were tapped for government service during the war effort, the Council's influence was limited until the Eisenhower Administration.

In 1962, the Business Council declared its independence. Responding in part to congressional and media criticisms of the Council's relationship with the government, the Kennedy administration asked the Council to include more small business representatives among its members and to allow reporters to cover its meetings. Rather than accept the conditions laid down by the administration, the Council severed its ties with the Commerce Department.

The Business Council has continued, however, to serve as a link between big business and the government. It adheres quite closely to its role as an advisory body, maintains a very low profile, and scrupulously avoids activities that might be interpreted as lobbying. The bulk of the Council's activities revolve around semiannual meetings, normally held at The Homestead in Hot Springs, Virginia. Here the full Council membership meets in private with high government officials and technical experts, in and out of government, to discuss economic policy issues and the business leaders' economic expectations. The Council also holds two Washington briefings each year. Between formal meetings, Council members are in frequent contact with the administration through liaison committees that consult informally with a variety of government departments. A very small staff organizes the Council's activities, coordinates the agendas of the meetings, processes suggestions for new members, and arranges visits of Council members to Washington.

The Council's membership is limited to 65 chief executive officers of the top industrial, retail, transportation, and financial corporations in the country. After five years, active members automatically "graduate," but they may reapply for active status after a one-year lapse. All members achieve "honorary" status when they turn seventy. There is an elaborate membership selection process, and an attempt is made to recruit members from all sections of the country. Though the Council denies that certain corporations informally have been assigned permanent seats in the organization, the chief executives of General Motors, Exxon, General Electric, DuPont, and a few others have been members since the Council's inception.

The Council's influence is primarily a function of the personal prestige of its members, and its status as a non-lobby means that it exerts more influence with the executive branch than with Congress. The degree of its influence depends as much upon the personality and orientation of the president as upon what party is in power. Lyndon Johnson, for example, courted the Council assiduously, whereas John Kennedy and Ronald Reagan kept their distance, although for different reasons. That the Council is influential is clear from the number of members who have been appointed to top executive or advisory positions in every administration.

Though the Council never formally takes a position on issues, the views of its members are nonetheless made known to government policymakers. When there is a consensus among members of the Business Council, it is often expressed through the Business Roundtable, an equally influential business organization that, unlike the Council, does take stands and does lobby for them. The membership overlap of the Business Council and the Business Roundtable is so extensive that one Business Council chairman declared: "We leave the advocacy to the Business Roundtable."[7] The Washington director of the Business Roundtable insisted that the Council and the Business Roundtable have no institutional ties but has also added that, "I guess on the outside, when you're dealing with one, you're dealing with the other."[8]

Committee for Economic Development

The Committee for Economic Development was intended by its founders to respond to emerging economic problems and government operations with new approaches that would be acceptable to the business community. In developing its positions, it has relied heavily on academic expertise, forging a union of the ivory tower and the marketplace. For nearly four decades, the CED has lived up to its goal, maintaining a unique position among business organizations by shunning the overt business advocacy of the NAM and the Chamber and by not limiting its concerns to bread-and-butter issues. It has also avoided the aloofness and obscurantism that frequently characterize the products of research think tanks. The CED involves corporate executives directly and extensively in deliberations that result in formal policy statements on key issues. The CED is incorporated as a nonprofit research and educational organization and prides itself on being "independent, non-partisan, and nonpolitical." The Committee also prides itself on the fact that its trustees "leave their company cloaks outside CED doors when they deliberate on committee policies."[9] As a rule, when the trustees testify for the CED, they do so without reference to their companies' interests.

The CED is generally thought to represent the most progressive wing of the business community. At the end of World War II, its founders argued that the old-line business organizations had not faced up to the evolving role of the federal government. With the depression of the 1930s still fresh in the minds of the CED's founders, the group's initial purpose was to help business executives plan for the postwar period to forestall a sharp economic decline and mass unemployment.

The CED was—and is—completely committed to the private enterprise system, though not to the laissez faire capitalism enshrined in the traditional business ideology. The founders of the organization believed that government intervention in the market was, in fact, necessary to insure the survival of the free enterprise system. Given the CED's origins, it is not surprising that it has been responsive, and frequently sympathetic, to the expanding government role in attacking the country's social ills. However, responding to conservative trends, the Committee's orientation has shifted, and now they are "placing greater emphasis on the role of the market system in achieving economic and social progress."[10] The CED has been sensitive to these charges, claiming that the shift reflects general societal attitudes. The trustees are less sanguine today than they were in the 1960s about their ability to prescribe remedies to intractable problems. The CED has consequently tended to concentrate on issues on which the trustees command expertise. The Committee nevertheless reaffirmed in 1982 its commitment to encouraging corporate involvement in social problems, "especially within communities where corporations do business."[11]

The CED is headquartered in New York, but its Washington office is growing in importance. Its 200 trustees are drawn mostly from the ranks of major corporations, with a sprinkling of university presidents and executives of other nonprofit organizations. The trustees work in a number of small study groups to formulate policy recommendations. They serve as individuals and are said not to be representatives of particular institutions. However, this distinction means little, as the personal views of corporate chief executives generally coincide with their companies' public pronouncements.

The CED Research Advisory Board, which is composed of outside economists and other social scientists as well as a few staff members, advises on the full range of CED research projects. Moreover, experts are selected to advise the trustees on each project the CED undertakes, and the prestige of the organization makes it easy to attract the most qualified help. The staff is primarily administrative, though senior staff members also serve as project directors.

The policy-formulation process is painstakingly careful, and proposed policy statements are meticulously scrutinized and undergo numerous drafts. The goal is consensus. As a result, the elapsed time from the formulation of a proposal until the release of the statement may be several years. The Research and Policy Committee, a group of some fifty trustees who meet together several times a year, monitors the progress of pending policy statements. Topics can be suggested by members of this committee or any other trustee, outside adviser, or staff member. Once the committee approves a topic for study, it sponsors a symposium at which the key elements of the problem are outlined. Following this, research is undertaken by a subcommittee of trustees, with the help of its advisory group and the CED staff. Draft reports are sent to the Research and Policy Committee, which may amend, approve, or return them to the subcommittee for redrafting. Finally, each trustee is free to add ''memoranda of comment, reservation or dissent'' to policy studies, thus allowing an airing of diverse views. Also, each statement contains a disclaimer absolving individual members from responsibility for views expressed in the policy statement.

This lengthy gestation period necessarily influences the topics the CED undertakes to study, but once released the policy statements are assured of a hearing and media attention. Although it does not lobby, the CED's policy statements may have considerable impact, as illustrated by its 1978 study, *Jobs for the Hard-to-Employ*. The policy statement reviewed the probable consequences of unemployment and provided an inventory of the segments of the labor force that were being hurt the most. The policy statement proposed ways in which the private sector could become a more active partner in government-sponsored employment and training efforts. Lastly, the statement detailed the types of institutions that would have to be created to actualize any public-private partnership in this area. When the Comprehensive Employment and Training Act was up for congressional reauthorization in 1978, both the Carter administration and lawmakers tapped the CED's expertise and experience in adding a new provision making private sector participation an integral part of federally funded training programs.

The CED's work has been well respected in the executive branch, where a number of former CED trustees and staffers have served in every administration in full-time or advisory capacities. The CED reports are also well thought of in business and university circles, both because of the high quality of their analysis and research and because of the personal reputations of the individuals involved in producing them.

Historically, criticism of the CED has come mainly from the more conservative segments of the business community, who have viewed CED trustees suspiciously as "do-gooders," or even as having been co-opted by the welfare state. On this account, the status of the CED in the Reagan administration may have suffered. The CED cannot be insensitive to what has been called "mainstream business opinion" because it is dependent upon private voluntary contributions from business and industry (including corporations not represented on its board of trustees) as well as from foundations and individuals. CED supporters have been known to tighten their purse strings when they felt that the Committee had wandered too far from prevailing business views, such as in its aborted 1961 policy statement on national labor policy.[12] Some trustees apparently thought that the study committee, which included some of the most prestigious academic industrial relations experts, went too far, particularly in recommending the expansion of union security provisions. True to its commitment to free expression, the CED published the report it sponsored—but not as a policy statement by the CED trustees. Even without the official imprimatur of the organization, the report, prepared by a prestigious academic group directed by George P. Shultz, later Secretary of Labor and the Treasury under Nixon and Secretary of State under Reagan, received widespread attention. The CED as an institution does not lobby, but its pronouncements have a long-term educational effect.

The Business Roundtable

The Business Roundtable, founded in 1972, is the youngest—but not least influential—of the major national business organizations. Like the older groups, it was established to meet a need that its organizers felt was not being adequately met by the existing business lobbies. The Chamber was perceived as an inadequate vehicle for big business concerns because of its sizeable small business constituency, and some of the corporate leaders objected to the approach of both the Chamber and the NAM on the grounds that they were too "shrill" and put forward "knee jerk conservative views." Moreover, for both the Chamber and the NAM, the diversity of interests represented and membership size resulted in rather slow decisionmaking and difficulties in focusing business lobbying efforts.[13]

The Business Roundtable was organized primarily to give big business more clout in Washington. As the role of the federal government expanded in the

1960s, the heads of leading business executive associations felt that the stakes were becoming too high to rely exclusively on such hired hands (or mouthpieces) as professional lobbyists to do their bidding in Washington. The CEOs decided that the game was worth personal attention and entered the fray.

For these reasons, the Roundtable was set up as an exclusive fraternity of the most powerful and prestigious national business leaders. It actively involves CEOs in the presentation of the "business story" to Congress, the White House, and other top governmental officials. Until the Roundtable's formation, few CEOs lobbied government directly, and when they did, they usually concentrated on their own companies' problems rather than the concerns of the larger business community.[14] Many Business Council members have also joined the Roundtable. Although overlap in the membership of these organizations makes them somewhat indistinguishable, the founders of the Roundtable wanted to maintain a distinction between their roles on the Council, which acts as a deliberative body, and on the new organization, which unabashedly lobbies. The Roundtable members have been quite successful in their new activist role. Doors on the Hill and in the White House are open to them as official Roundtable representatives, and there is no record that Roundtable members ever had to picket on the outside to present their views.

Since its creation, the Roundtable's membership has grown to about 200. It includes the CEOs of the top industrial, financial, and commercial companies in the country. Distinguished as its membership is, the Roundtable does not voluntarily publish the list; according to a 1979 unofficial listing, there were 192 members. They represented the 10 largest corporations in the 1980 Fortune 500 list; 21 of the top 25, 40 of the top 50, 70 of the top 100, 113 of the top 200, and 131 of the top 500.[15] Membership is by invitation only, as befits the exclusivity of the club, and there has been no shortage of executives waiting for the call.

The Business Roundtable had its origins in three earlier organizations—the Labor Law Study Group, the Construction Users Anti-Inflation Roundtable, and the March Group—each of which brought to the Roundtable different priorities and different approaches. The Labor Law Study Group was formed in 1965 in response to organized labor's attempt to repeal section 14(b) of the Taft-Hartley Act, which provides for precedence of state laws forbidding a union shop (so-called right-to-work laws) over federal law, which permits it. According to Virgil Day, former vice-president of General Electric, the founders of the organization thought that management should take the initiative in the formulation of labor law rather than react to union proposals: "It occurred to us that it might be useful to see if it wouldn't be possible to reverse the process of always waiting until we had to meet some union pressure. So we decided it would be worth a try."[16]

Fifty companies, representing a broad cross section of industry, joined the

Group, and forty associations, including the NAM and the Chamber, backed its activities. They brought together a number of leading labor lawyers to draft amendments to the National Labor Relations Act and to meet privately with government officials. Though they succeeded in drumming up within the business community considerable interest in "union abuses," they did not succeed in convincing the Nixon administration of the need to amend the NLRA.

Shortages in skilled labor amid rising construction costs in the late 1960s led to the organization of the Construction Users Anti-Inflation Roundtable (CUAR) in 1969. At the urging of the NAM and the Chamber, construction users and contractors formed an alliance to arrest the rising costs of labor in the building trades. Headed by Roger Blough, former chairman of both the Business Council and U.S. Steel, CUAR attracted a membership of 100 companies and established an organizational structure that would eventually be adopted by the Business Roundtable. Its strategy was multifaceted. It cooperated with the Labor Law Study Group in its litigation campaign to reduce union power through the courts, and it undertook a regional multicontractor-multitrade bargaining strategy to overcome fragmentation in the industry. Furthermore, it coordinated local user action and set up an extensive information system in order to reduce competition among firms for construction labor. It also joined with other business groups in opposing common situs picketing bills pending before Congress and favored the repeal of federal and state prevailing wage legislation in construction.

In 1972, the CUAR and the Labor Law Study Group merged. Since there was considerable overlap in their membership and their aims were similar, the merged organization benefited from economies of size.

The March Group, the third organization antecedent to the Business Roundtable, most closely embodied the concept behind the present-day Roundtable. Originally composed of CEOs who had long been active in the Business Council, the immediate spur to its formation was the Nixon administration's implementation of an unprecedented peacetime program of wage and price controls. In response to suggestions by Federal Reserve Board Chairman Arthur Burns and Treasury Secretary John Connally that business improve its representation in Washington, a dozen corporate chief executives met in March 1972 to present an authoritative business voice on national economic policies.

The March Group was initially intended to remain a very exclusive, tightly knit group of about fifteen chief executive officers. They would work behind the scenes and take no public stands. It was expected that established business organizations, such as the Chamber and the NAM, would be asked to channel the group's views to the appropriate decisionmakers. A great many business leaders wanted to get into the act, however, and within a year the March Group had 100 members. The merger with the CUAR and the Labor Law Study Group followed in 1973. About two-thirds of the corporate members of the March Group were already associated with the other groups. The new organization, which became known as the Business Roundtable, not only expanded and absorbed most of the programs of the three groups, but committed considerable resources to areas other than construction, litigation, and lobbying. One of the more publicized efforts was an educational program presenting the Round-table's views about the working of the American economy.

At the time of the merger with the CUAR and the Labor Law Study Group, some members of the March Group argued that the organization was making a mistake by getting itself involved in the ideological struggle against labor. They were concerned that the merger threatened to embroil the Roundtable in public controversy, and might tarnish its public image by identifying the organization as another lobby representing business interests. However, the members of the CUAR and the Labor Law Study Group were not willing to give up their special concerns with wage policies and labor law. In order not to lose their identity, they reorganized into subsidiary units within the larger organization.

Unlike the NAM and the Chamber, whose professional staffs have considerable influence over the agenda and even the direction the organization takes, the Business Roundtable is run by its members. The main organizational components of the Roundtable are a small executive committee, a larger policy committee, and a number of task forces—sixteen as of mid-1982—that have responsibility for research and lobbying in specific policy areas. The agenda of the Roundtable generally reflects dominant issues on the government's agenda as well as the needs and interests of individual members. To minimize conflict, the Roundtable has generally tried to steer clear of single-industry issues.

The table may be round, but certain knights of industry tend to be more equal than others. About twenty firms have been invariably represented on the Roundtable policy committee, including AT&T, Alcoa, DuPont, Exxon, GE, GM, IBM, Sears Roebuck, Union Carbide, and U.S. Steel. The balance is composed of the 170 or so corporations who are not "permanent" members of the policy committee. Aside from personal contacts, the "rank and file" members can influence policy on the task forces on which they serve, and selection of a given task force is likely to reflect members' special interests. In addition, informal polls are taken of knowledgeable or concerned members of the Roundtable if their concern with an issue is known to members of the policy committee, and, as in any exclusive club, members are free to "lobby" their peers who sit on the policy committee.

Task forces normally appoint a lead member who coordinates the research on the topic of concern and lobbies on bills that are in the task force's jurisdiction. The chairman normally recruits assistants from his (there are no women in the Roundtable) own corporation or borrows them from the staffs of other Round-table companies. Roundtable members tend to rely heavily on the expertise of their Washington representatives. The task forces are also aided by outside experts who are hired for particular projects.

Because of this heavy reliance on personnel from member corporations, the Roundtable's own staff is very small. The organization's funds come entirely from annual dues, which range from $2,600 to $42,000, based upon stockholders' equity and gross sales. The Roundtable's main office is in New York, close to the corporate headquarters of numerous member companies. The small permanent Washington staff tracks key issues for the task forces and coordinates the efforts of Washington representatives and the CEOs of member corporations when the Roundtable mobilizes on a bill.

The decisive advantage of the Roundtable is the direct access to high level policymakers it enjoys by virtue of its members' positions as the most powerful business leaders in the country. According to one observer:

> The Business Roundtable almost seems to be a belated recognition of
> the frequently demonstrated historical principal that royalty always
> commands more attention, respect, and awe than the lesser nobility.
> Neither the National Association of Manufacturers nor the U.S.
> Chamber of Commerce can do what a uniquely conceived and spe-
> cially powered lobby of the largest and most responsible economic
> interests in the country can achieve.[17]

Under the Reagan administration, however, the Roundtable's status in Washington circles has diminished slightly. The name of the game is no longer access, but influence. Business representatives do not have trouble getting appointments at the White House, as in previous administrations; now the question is, What do they offer? The Roundtable cannot offer the kind of grass-roots organization on which the Reagan administration has come to depend heavily. Moreover, business leaders have not been wildly enthusiastic in their support of Reaganomics and some of its publicly questioned consequences.

The Business Roundtable has developed a low-key approach typified by pragmatism and willingness to compromise. Roundtable members work quietly behind the scenes rather than in public—they testify at public hearings rather infrequently. Their nonpublic approach to lobbying gives them greater flexibility in their dealings with policymakers than they would have if they were to take public stands on issues. Although other organizations, particularly the NAM and the Chamber, have tried to moderate their positions and to approach issues in a more positive way than they have traditionally done, the Roundtable has been more successful at it, and has been perceived as being correspondingly more effective in achieving its legislative goals. Currently, however, a moderate position may be less well received by the Reagan White House than a hard-line management view.

The relative success achieved by the Roundtable has not been without costs. For example, the Roundtable has had a somewhat uneasy relationship with other segments of the business community, particularly with the NAM, the Chamber, and the small business lobby. It has been roundly criticized by all three for being too quick to compromise and for an unwillingness to fight tough battles that might produce legislation more favorable to business interests and more closely aligned with free market principles. Lobbyists for the Chamber and the NAM, who tend to take rather hard-line and rigid stands on some issues, have criticized the Roundtable for "naively cutting deals with the Administration" that cannot be kept in Congress.[18] The National Federation of Independent Business has even condemned the Roundtable for "sucking eggs with the president."[19] (These comments were made before the advent of the Reagan administration.)

Other business organizations have also criticized the Roundtable for ducking difficult issues, such as food stamps for strikers. The Roundtable maintains that it can only deal with a limited number of issues because the work is done directly by the CEOs, who have pressing time constraints on engaging in "good works" outside their own corporations. The number of priority issues the organization has chosen to deal with has been slowly increasing, but the Roundtable is nevertheless open to the criticism that it only takes on the issues it thinks it can win and avoids the issues that will give it bad press. Also, there is some resentment toward the Roundtable because it draws on Chamber and NAM research and other staff resources but does not necessarily coordinate its lobbying with these organizations.

The Chamber has been particularly vexed by the Roundtable's efforts, apparently because the Roundtable has threatened its position as "the voice of business." This is all the more true now that business roundtables are being founded to represent the large companies at the state level. Though they are not directly affiliated with the national Business Roundtable, the national organization did help them to get started and has encouraged them. At the end of 1982 there were roundtables in California, Massachusetts, and Minnesota. Nevertheless, speculation that these state organizations could be the beginning of a nationwide network that could potentially rival the Chamber's federated structure remains unfounded.

The Business Roundtable's relations with small and medium-sized business have been strained because there is some sentiment among the latter that some Roundtable victories have been won at their expense. There are considerable ideological differences and fundamental conflicts between the two business groups and, of course, different priorities, which some actions by the big business group could not help but exacerbate. The "smalls," for example, tend to take a harder line when it comes to resisting federal regulation. They argue that since they have far fewer resources than the large corporations, the paperwork that regulation imposes puts them at an unfair disadvantage vis-à-vis their larger competitors. Smaller businesses are also less likely to be unionized than larger companies and so tend to feel more strongly about fighting unionism.

The Roundtable is sensitive to the problem of its troubled relations with small business organizations. However, maintaining ties with the rest of the business community will not be easy for the Roundtable. American business is no monolith. This was brought home by the launching of a new business lobby called the American Business Conference, which is modeled on the Roundtable but actually seeks to limit the latter's influence. It was founded in December 1980 by American Stock Exchange Chairman Arthur Levitt, Jr. Its membership is restricted to 100 CEOs of high-growth, mid-sized companies, many of whom have voiced impatience with the Roundtable's pragmatism and alleged lack of commitment to supply side tenets. In 1982, however, ABC forsook the true faith and took an active role in lobbying for President Reagan's tax increase.

Small Business

Like their bigger brethren (and for some of the same reasons), the small business lobbyists have experienced considerable growth in numbers and sophistication in the past decade. The increased sensitivity of government to small business's concerns is due in large part to this development of small business organization and the increase in the visibility of the "smalls" in Washington and within the business community generally. Defending small business is, like motherhood, always popular with the voters.

Small business activism dates from the effort in the late 1940s to create and maintain the House and Senate Small Business Committees. However, the spur to the intense efforts on the part of small business in recent years has been the dramatic increase in government intervention. Many small business executives claim that regulations, particularly those in the equal employment and health and safety fields, impose excessive burdens on everyday operations.

Small business organizations have recently experienced dramatic growth, especially considering small businessmen's traditional difficulty in organizing on a national scale. The relative lag in representation for small business in Washington has been due in the main to its diversity and to the fact that problems of small business tend to be local in nature (as are most of their product and labor markets). The increase in federal regulation has generated national problems for small business. As noted earlier, the NAM and the Chamber, despite their predominantly small business memberships, tend not to reflect clearly the concerns of small business. Small business, even more than big business, has found these two mass membership organizations to be subject to too many crosscurrents and pressures from too many competing groups. The only means of assuring that their own views are heard clearly by policymakers has been to establish organizations that represent them exclusively.

Small business is represented at the federal level by several organizations. The number of different bodies purporting to speak for the small businessman is indicative of the lack of unity within the small business community. By far the largest organization is the National Federation of Independent Business, with a membership of about 470,000 firms, accounting for over one of every three business firms with annual receipts in excess of $50,000. Nearly half of its members are retailers and providers of nonprofessional services. Construction and manufacturing account for a fourth of the membership, and the balance is in wholesaling, finance, professional services, and agriculture. Founded in 1943 to represent exclusively the interests of independent businesses and the self-employed, the NFIB remained largely a paper organization until the 1970s. Though there are no formal limits as to size, almost two-thirds of NFIB members employ fewer than ten people, and over eighty percent of its total membership employ fewer than twenty people. Most of NFIB's growth occurred in the 1970s. Only a small part of its resources is centered in Washington. In 1981, the Washington office employed fourteen staff members, while the home office in San Mateo, California, employed approximately 100. There were 565 field personnel around the country, and thirty-six lobbyists in state capitals. The organization's funding comes from dues, ranging from $35 to $500 annually and yielding the national office a budget of approximately $6.5 million for 1981.

The NFIB regularly polls its membership using questionnaires called "mandates," which are published in the newsletter it issues eight times a year. The results of the mandates form the basis of NFIB official policy and are reported to members of Congress and officials in the executive branch. These democratically adopted mandates are binding on the NFIB, and this often prevents federation lobbyists from committing their organization to proposed policy compromises. The NFIB also rates members of Congress on key small business issues and uses these ratings in its determinations of whom to support with its PAC resources. The NFIB-PAC spent over $218,000 in the 1980 election cycle, but the direct funding of political candidates accounts for only a fraction of its influence. It is noted for its aggressive political and lobbying strategy and the use of its grass roots.

The NFIB's rival for the title of the small business voice is the National Small Business Association (NSB). Founded in 1937, the NSB claims approximately 50,000 member companies. In the mid-1970s, there was some talk of merging NSB with the Federation as the NSB's finances were shaky. The Association has since regained its stability, and the merger idea has been rejected.

The NSB compensates for its relatively small membership by lobbying in conjunction with the Small Business Legislative Council (SBLC). The NSB, along with about twenty trade associations, started the SBLC in 1977 as an ad hoc response to the passage of the 1936 Robinson-Patman Act. The SBLC has, since then, become a permanent means of broadening the NSB's base for determining policy and coordinating lobbying on behalf of small business. Membership in SBLC is open both to national trade and professional associations and to regional and state associations whose members are predominantly small businesses or independent professionals. The SBLC allows considerable autonomy to each member association. The Council can take a position on an issue only when 60 percent of its members agree. Moreover, once a decision is taken, each member association may support the policy and allow its name to be used on Council statements. Each member is also free to oppose publicly any policy the SBLC has taken if that member's organizational interests are in conflict with the SBLC's position. The degree of flexibility with which the council operates is essential to the maintenance of the coalition and is also reflective of the multiplicity of different interests within the small business community. To sell its services, the SBLC claims:

> In the past, the small business community has too often been frag-
> mented and defensive in posture. . . . As a result, small business has
> been out-played in Washington for the last 30 years by big business,
> big government, big labor and more recently by so-called spokesmen
> for the consumer and a variety of related groups.
>   SBLC turns this around.[20]

The Council of Small and Independent Business Associations (COSIBA) is another umbrella organization of small business associations. It includes members from the NSB, National Association of Small Business Investment Companies, National Business League (which represents about 15,000 minority business enterprises), and five regional small business associations. The NFIB withdrew from the organization in October 1982. Created in the late 1970s as a vehicle for the coordination of small business's efforts to win the employment tax credit, COSIBA claims to represent one million small businesses. Because its membership represents such diverse interests, COSIBA has experienced difficulty securing a consensus on issues to be tackled, lacking as it does the flexibility of the SBLC. For this reason, COSIBA serves more as a forum for the exchange of information on legislative developments and for contacts between the main small business organizations and administration officials than as a coordinating body for legislative action.

The tensions between the NFIB and the NSB stem in the main from their competition for members, but are also due to significant differences in policy and style. The NFIB is known to side more frequently with the big business interests than the NSB and has been criticized for this by the NSB. One example of this split was the reaction in 1981 to the 10–5–3 proposal for rapid depreciation write-offs. While the NFIB supported the proposal, the NSB opposed it as a giveaway to big business and argued that its total cost would be inflationary.

The NFIB is generally considered to be more effective as a lobbying organization than the NSB, mainly because its larger membership and more secure financial base have enabled it to mount better organized, staffed, and financed campaigns. Recently, however, the NFIB's aggressiveness has irked legislators who have been poorly rated by the organization but consider themselves major defenders of "the little guys." The NSB does not employ such an explicit "reward and punish" strategy; its style is more low-key and sophisticated. This dedication to flexibility accounts for the failure of NSB to form a PAC which would involve the organization in formal commitments.

Defenders of NFIB's style of operation suggest that the organization's effectiveness is linked to its willingness to cooperate with big business interests in order to influence Congress. Given the limited resources available to smaller business, its representation, so the argument goes, must rely on the well-heeled big business organizations to deliver the message to the halls of government. If this argument has merit, it would appear that much of the touted "small business clout" has not met the test of the political marketplace. Politicians may love small business, but the $218,000 that NFIB-PAC collected in the 1980 national electon can buy few votes. Nonetheless, small business organizations, whether on their own or with the support of big business, can play an important role, as the 1978 campaign against the labor law reform bill demonstrated.

It would be a mistake, therefore, to discount the potential influence of small business organizations. Lawmakers have recently been paying more attention to small businessmen, and not only because of their more effective organization and more sophisticated lobbying efforts. Small businesses number between 4.5 and 11 million—depending upon the definition used—and constitute a natural grass-roots constituency. Also, many members of Congress have backgrounds in small business and a built-in sensitivity to the problems faced by small entrepreneurs. Furthermore, starting out in business for oneself is a hallowed national tradition, and therefore a legislator's public support of small business priorities generally gets better press than backing the interests of multinational corporations. Finally, the organizations representing small businesses have achieved some momentum and have succeeded in making known the important economic role small businesses play.

Small business organization has recently led to some significant legislative successes. In 1978, the small business lobby was for the first time able to take some credit for a number of major successes, such as the defeat of the labor law reform bill and the consumer protection agency. Since then, albeit with a strong assist from the "bigs," small business has been winning increasing support for its position that government regulation of business imposes unfair costs on smaller enterprises. The small business community was made more visible by the January 1980 White House Conference on Small Business, and it has played a role in the passage of the 1981 tax and budget bills.

Even though the "bigs" and "smalls" do not necessarily share the same destination, organizations representing larger business interests occasionally take advantage of the ride offered by small business. This is one explanation for the Chamber's decision in 1976 to establish the Center for Small Business and the Council for Small Business. Moreover, observers have commented that "the big business organizations and companies are fairly adept at aligning their issues with small business . . . and sort of hiding behind them."[21]

Whereas the big business community can capitalize on the recent momentum gathered by small business, small business is still relatively dependent on the help of the larger business interests to win many of its battles. The smalls do not have the financial backing to be economically independent. As they continue to seek to expand the scope of their independent lobbying and to push their own legislative agendas, they must be sensitive to the priorities of the Chamber, the NAM, and the Roundtable. Only on rare occasions do the small business lobbies advocate positions opposed by the big business interests. Stands against big business can serve to impress the membership with the importance of separate representation, but the small business lobbies cannot afford to indulge too frequently in such luxuries.

All in the Family

In addition to the major national general purpose employer organizations, trade and industry associations have played a key role in the revitalization of the business community's legislative prowess. Aid has also come from the Washington offices and public affairs departments of corporations and from sympathetic single issue citizens' groups. Further help has been provided by the renaissance of the conservative research industry, largely funded by the same business interests that are picking up the tab for the rejuvenation and expansion of the employer community's lobbying efforts. The Conference Board is a nonpartisan organization with a solid research record of more than three score years. The American Enterprise Institute (AEI) is a right-of-center think tank providing much of the innovation, research, and analysis behind the effort to regain the so-called business paradise lost. The Institute of Contemporary Studies is similar to AEI, but with smaller resources and influence. The Heritage Foundation is a relatively new conservative think tank whose research rarely strays from traditional conservative ideology.

Trade Associations

Trade associations have traditionally served American business as centers for concerted activity. Special interests within the broader employer community have been increasingly well represented over the past decade by trade and industry associations. Approximately 30 percent of the 5,800 nationwide trade associations are now headquartered in Washington—more than any other city, including New York. In the 1970s, trade associations flocked to the capital in record numbers, reflecting the increased impact of government decisions on industries and the consequent need to communicate with and influence federal policymakers and program administrators.[22]

Membership in national trade and industry associations has grown as companies have found that the mass-membership organizations, such as the Chamber and the NAM, have so many competing interests that the particular needs of specific industries are often overlooked.[23] Companies need the specialized monitoring, research, and lobbying services provided by trade associations in order to deal specifically with the public policy questions that impinge directly on their operations.

Trade associations provide other services as well, including public relations, new product research, the setting of quality and certification standards, and the compilation of statistics on market conditions, salaries, wages, hours, employee benefits, and other questions. Although some organizations offer labor relations programs—including seminars on labor-management relations, advising members on long-term management strategy, and keeping them up to date on recent developments in the field—relatively few organizations get directly involved in their members' collective bargaining.

Trade and industry associations come in all shapes and sizes. They range from the giant, such as the American Petroleum Institute, an umbrella organization of associations representing the diverse sectors of the oil industry, to the obscure, such as the Frozen Onion Ring Packers' Council. They have different structures, styles, objectives, and vastly different resources at their disposal. The priorities of these organizations frequently shift with time, reflecting both their members' needs and the government's agenda, but some retain a consistent program. Firms engaged in multiemployer bargaining normally establish a separate entity exclusively for collective bargaining purposes (such as the Bituminous Coal Operators Association) which may or may not also offer the range of services provided by other national trade and industry associations. The main organizations of the construction industry, the Association of General Contractors and the Associated Builders and Contractors, have been preoccupied with labor issues. Other labor policy areas elicit the sustained interest of different trade and industry organizations. For example, the Chemical Manufacturers Association has an intense interest in occupational safety and health.

The Association of General Contractors (AGC) is the preeminent construction employers' organization in Washington. It claims a membership of more than 8,000 general contracting firms and 20,000 associate and affiliate members. Founded in 1918 in response to President Woodrow Wilson's appeal for the formation of a national organization through which the government could deal with the construction industry, it has developed a considerable grass-roots organization based on 113 chapters and a national staff of ninety people, of whom nineteen are registered lobbyists. It provides a wide range of services to its members, including education, research, and governmental relations services in the areas of equal opportunity, manpower and training, and safety and health. Approximately half of the AGC's members are union contractors and half operate open shops. The AGC straddles that divide with staff divisions devoted to collective bargaining services and open shop services. Its promotional pamphlet strives to give both sections of its membership equal billing. On the one hand:

> Since the Association's founding and the establishment of its labor policy, it has striven by original and innovative means to develop and maintain an effective, productive working relationship with the building and construction trades unions.

It goes on to say:

> Since its formation, AGC has served and protected the interests of its open shop members and those segments of the industry that choose not to work with collective bargaining agreements. The Association has long recognized that management's right to manage is paralleled by the right-to-work privilege of employees.

The Associated Builders and Contractors has never been that even-handed. Founded in 1950 by a group of Baltimore contractors "fed up with taking orders from union foremen and business agents," it is the primary voice for open shop contractors in Washington.[24] It states in a "fact sheet" that its primary goal is "to promote the Merit Shop throughout the construction industry. . . . In a Merit Shop firm, employees have the right to belong or not belong to a union, and to further their skills and individual ambitions." Though the ABC publicly insists that it is not antiunion but pro–Merit Shop, it is widely regarded by the union movement as a union-busting organization. The ABC has 17,500 members and offers a somewhat narrower range of member services than does the AGC. Its top priority is the repeal of the Davis-Bacon Act, which requires that prevailing area wages established by the Secretary of Labor be paid on all federal and federally assisted construction contracts in excess of $2,000. The ABC position is that the outmoded act inflates the cost of government construction.

Single Issue Groups

In addition to trade and industry associations, management has organized around specific issue areas. These single issue organizations vary greatly in organization, makeup, and working techniques, but they all serve to represent employers' views to federal policymakers. UBA, the ERISA Industry Committee (ERIC), and the Right to Work Committee illustrate the diversity in style and operations of single issue organizations representing business interests. UBA operates mostly as an adviser and consultant to member corporations that do their own lobbying. ERIC is a policymaking and lobbying organization representing a group of major companies. And the National Right to Work Committee is an activist, grass-roots organization generally associated with employer interests.

UBA (formerly Unemployment Benefit Advisers), established in 1933, is a group of experts on unemployment and workmen's compensation. It undertakes research in the field; acts as a clearinghouse of information for employers, their associations, and government administrators; publishes bulletins; and coordinates members' lobbying efforts on Capitol Hill. UBA takes no formal policy positions itself.

ERIC, established in 1977, is a different kind of single issue organization. It was organized first as a forum in which major corporate employee benefit plan sponsors could exchange views on various regulatory and legislative proposals relating to the 1974 employee retirement law, and second to present ERISA's views to the relevant executive agencies and to Congress. ERIC has also filed friend of the court briefs in ERISA-related litigation. It has no full-time staff and is run out of the offices of a Washington law firm; the bulk of the members' fees is used to keep the firm on retainer.

A third kind of single issue organization in the labor field is the National Right-to-Work Committee. Founded in 1955, its primary goal has been to oppose the union shop. Though its rather militant stand is generally thought to represent a management perspective, it is not formally a representative business organization. It operates as a citizens' organization and claims a membership of 1.5 million people whom it solicits and rallies through an extensive direct mail operation. The Committee and its legal arm, the National Right-to-Work Legal Defense Foundation, operate on an $8 million budget and employ a staff of over a hundred. Because of the Committee's militancy, the mainstream employers' organizations try to distance themselves publicly, although the Committee has cooperated in legislative campaigns.

The Research Industry

The various business organizations are supported by a growing research community that provides analytical backup for the executives and association staff on the front lines. In recent years, the scope and quality of policy research used by the business community have vastly improved. Employer representatives have learned to draw on the expertise of sympathetic university academics as well as the resources of specialized think tank organizations.

The Conference Board, founded in 1916, is the oldest and the largest employer research organization. It undertakes research projects to meet the needs of its more than 4000 associates (who are mainly corporations and trade associations, with a sprinkling of universities, government agencies, and trade unions). The Board's research has focused on areas where managers have to make decisions most frequently: strategic planning, marketing and financial management, corporate governance, compensation, business trends, and industrial relations. However, in recent years, the Board has paid more attention to outside forces affecting corporate operations, such as urban problems, government regulation, and antitrust matters. This reflects increased business concern with public policy. The primary purpose of the Conference Board is to improve the decisionmaking of managers by providing them with necessary information. The Board also aims to improve public understanding of management and economics so that the public can better evaluate the performance of business.

In contrast to the Conference Board, whose research focuses on business operations, the American Enterprise Institute for Public Policy Research focuses on public policy issues. It is the largest, best-established, and most broadly based conservative not-for-profit research and education institute in Washington. Founded in 1943 with a staff of five, it has grown to have a budget of almost $10 million and a staff of 138 in 1980. The Institute's studies cover the gamut of federal policies and attempt to be responsive to current issues. The Institute also publishes a number of periodicals and hosts seminars on policy issues for executives, journalists, government officials, and visiting scholars. It has very close ties—especially financial and ideological—to the business community, and corporate representation on its board of trustees. Although the Institute's approach to economic issues remains staunchly conservative, the organization justly prides itself on favoring the competition of ideas. It happens that conservative views usually prevail in the Institute's publications and findings, but its staff is certainly not muzzled. Some of the most cogent criticism of Reagan administration supply side theology was penned by AEI economists.

It has been said that "if AEI made it acceptable to be a conservative, Heritage has made it popular."[25] Although both organizations are frequently linked with conservative thought, there is a wide gulf between the two in the quality of their research and their approach to public policy issues. Heritage Foundation, founded in 1973 with $250,000 from Colorado brewer Joseph Coors, is the new kid on the block in the research community. With a budget of $7 million and a full-time staff of ninety people, Heritage puts out analyses of policy issues and publishes a number of journals and newsletters. Heritage Foundation's style is less analytical than AEI's. Its conclusions and recommendations are predictable and reflect the views of the political right on the public policy issues of the moment. It is highly visible, places considerable emphasis on its public information functions, and is known as President Reagan's favorite think tank.

In addition to these general purpose research organizations, specialized institutes, such as the Employee Benefits Research Institute in Washington and the Center on National Labor Policy in Virginia, focus on particular issue areas. All these groups provide an important commodity to the business lobby, whether it be fresh ideas or old wine in new bottles. Their growth in the past decade is a significant, if belated, recognition on the part of the business establishment of the importance of facts, figures, and analysis for bolstering traditional business positions and selling them to legislators and the public.

4

Getting the Act Together

"Please sir, may I have more?"
—Charles Dickens, *Oliver Twist*

New Tactics

In the years since Justice Lewis F. Powell wrote his memorandum to the U.S. Chamber of Commerce on how to restore the business community's public image, employer lobbies have made great strides in the legislative arena. Though clearly related to complex social and economic trends, the position of advantage business holds on Capitol Hill is nonetheless a direct product of a concerted effort by business leaders to devote more of their attention to politics and public policy.

During the 1970s and early 1980s business has vastly expanded activities in Washington. Hundreds of trade associations, representing specific industry interests, have sprung up in the District or moved there from other locations. The Business Roundtable, whose trademark is the direct participation of corporate chief executive officers, was founded in 1972. Two years later the NAM moved its headquarters from New York to Washington. The membership of the national Chamber doubled between 1981 and 1982; its grass-roots organization and its communications capabilities grew to include a multimillion-dollar satellite communications network. In the mid-1970s, the National Federation of Independent Business increased the size of its Washington operations. Not only did business devote added resources to influencing government, but it also learned how to use them better.

Faced with a vast array of new regulations, business found it advisable, indeed essential, to expand its national lobbying capability. Company managers' styles were being substantially cramped by the public policymakers in Washington. Irving Shapiro, former chief executive officer of DuPont and past chairman of the Business Roundtable, expressed the new awareness succinctly: "You have zero chance of scoring points unless you get into the game."[1] Clearly, business leaders decided that the business of government is too important to leave in the hands of professional politicians.

The 1970s provided business lobbyists with new opportunities to influence policymakers. Internal congressional reforms fragmented power centers in Congress, reducing the power of committee chairmen and giving more influence to younger legislators independent of party leadership. Congress also experienced high turnover, and new members tended to be open to new ideas. Because they were independent of local political machines, they turned for support to direct mail, a marketing technique easily grasped by business for its own advantage.[2]

Most important, the 1970s brought a change in the campaign financing laws that offered new opportunities for business lobbying. The election finance reforms placed limits on a contributor's donation to a candidate, but they also provide a method to circumvent the limitations placed on political action committees (PACs). Employer organizations took full advantage of the new law and it has redounded decisively to the advantage of the business lobbies.

PACs have been created by almost every special interest lobby, and in 1982 they contributed some twenty-two percent of the $314 million spent by congressional candidates. Although unions pioneered in establishing PACs, business proved to be a quick learner and in the 1982 elections corporate and business-related trade association PACs raised $82 million to labor's $32 million.

Business PACs have included among their beneficiaries Democrats and Republicans, but it should not be surprising that the latter were favored, getting more than three of every five business PAC dollars. For example, in October 1982 the national Chamber published an "opportunity list" of 100 congressional races in which investment of political action committee contributions would be most cost-effective. *All* the favored candidates were Republican. The Chamber apparently could not find a single Democrat who deserved the organization's nod, whereas its "hit list" was made up exclusively of Democrats.[3] Some board members apparently questioned Lesher's inability to find a single righteous candidate in the Democrat fold. The Chamber's deputy political director, Neil Newhouse, explained the selection: "We've spent a lot of time trying to locate good strong Democrat conservatives. . . . We haven't been able to find any."[4] In contrast, labor PACs favored Democratic over Republican candidates by fourteen to one. PACs sponsored by neither business nor labor also played an active role. Indications are that conservative PACs make up the bulk of the ideologically directed contributions. The two richest ideological PACs in 1982 were the National Congressional Club (founded by Senator Jesse Helms of North Carolina) and the National Conservative Political Action Committee. But resources can be squandered, as the affluent lobbies demonstrated in 1982.

The major national employer organizations played only a minor role in raising money. Only the national Chamber and the National Federation of Independent Business have their own PACs. The National Chamber Alliance, rather than contributing cash to candidates, instructs its regional representatives and local business members to provide such services as research, fundraising, and advertising advice to candidates. The Roundtable relies on the sizeable sums contributed by its members' PACs, and the National Small Business Association eschews such a direct ''reward and punish strategy.''[5]The NAM has decided against establishing its own PAC and instead provides advisory services to member companies through its publication, the *PAC Manager*. The independent Business-Industry Political Action Committee, formed in 1963, is the most experienced organization advising corporations on how to handle their PACs.

Supply Side Economics

Political success in the United States depends on the ability to win the support of the center. Business lobbies have displayed a sophisticated understanding of this phenomenon. It is instructive to recall that in 1964 many, possibly a majority, of business leaders opposed Barry Goldwater, the leading conservative of the day. An estimated 60 percent of the Business Council members, for example, supported the Johnson-Humphrey ticket.[6] In the 1970s, though, the political center began to shift to the right, and business lobbyists were quick to follow.

New Promises

Since the Great Depression of the 1930s, presidents and most policymakers—whatever their rhetoric—have not viewed the economy as a rapidly self-adjusting and self-correcting cybernetic system. The invisible hand of the marketplace has been felt to require some government activity to promote macroeconomic stability. Despite frequent disagreements over fiscal and monetary policies, Republican as well as Democratic presidents have embraced the general principle that the federal government should play an active role in regulating the course of the economy. President Reagan has represented a major break in this perception of the governmental role, and one of his first acts in office was to rule out using active fiscal and monetary policies to promote social objectives.

Stripped of all its questionable calculus, the centerpiece of Reaganomics was supply side economics. According to this view, the private sector is inherently stable, and economic problems are primarily the result of an overactive government pursuing stop-and-go policies of demand management. If the central government would only keep tight and constant monetary policies, then the economy would rapidly prosper and all segments of society would benefit. It followed, according to the supply-siders, that the forces that had been blocking the dynamic potential had to be removed. They argued that government policies had muzzled private enterprise, holding back its growth potential. If taxes were lowered and nondefense spending sharply cut, rational expectations on the part of investors would result in vast increases in productivity, savings, and investment as well as aggregate growth. They predicted, moreover, that the federal budget deficit would melt in the sunshine generated by all this growth, as increased economic activity resulted in overflowing coffers at the federal treasury. Furthermore, all societal groups were expected to benefit because increased investment would spur increased employment, and inflation would be cut without a serious recession.

Sophisticated business lobbyists questioned the realism of this script, although they embraced it publicly—it presented an offer they could not refuse. Adjustment to the new economics was not easy. It brought into question the entire role of the welfare state, which many segments of business had long before learned to accommodate. "Public policy and social issues," said Reginald Jones, former chairman of General Electric, "are no longer adjuncts to business planning and management. They are in the mainstream of it."[7] Some employers opposed the overall intrusion of welfare capitalism from its inception; for others it became an acquired taste. Business developed an accommodating attitude toward federal intervention, fighting excesses and accepting handouts. For many companies, government intervention brought significant benefits, such as support for research and development efforts and increased demand for goods and services. However, most of the business community remained opposed to the new regulations. Antipollution laws are costly to many companies and equal opportunity, though acceptable in principle, interferes with well-established practices and freedom of action.

Gradually, the mixed economy and the welfare state came to be viewed by most segments of business as a smorgasbord from which they could pick and choose those morsels that promoted social stability and economic growth and improved profits for specific companies or industries. On balance, however, the business community never developed a taste for the welfare state. The main criterion determining a company's position on any single program was always the financial impact it would have.

In the late 1970s, business and its allies began a concerted push for rollbacks, arguing that interventionist government had gone too far. Of course, advocates of an expanding welfare state have insisted that past accomplishments have barely corrected old wrongs, and that the next step is to advance the New Deal and Great Society agendas. Since the 1980 election, however, the national debate has focused less on the need for compromise between the contending interests and more on the need for a radically new beginning and a reversal of the growth of government. How has business made the transition?

For some parts of the employer community, the beginning of the Reagan era heralded an ideological homecoming. Small business and the entrepreneurial organizations were among candidate Reagan's earliest supporters. They were—and are—also the backbone of the Republican party. The big business establishment and the financial community have been more recent converts to Reaganomics.[8] They have had to do some gear shifting to adjust to the new orientation of the national debate. These employers tend to be far less ideological and more pragmatic than the small employers, and have made their accommodations with the expanding role of government. Their interest in the status quo is obvious; they prefer stability to a totally unleashed free market. This segment of the business community favored John Connally and then George Bush in the 1980 primaries until it became clear that Reagan would be the Republican presidential nominee.

Many business leaders who jumped on the Reaganomics bandwagon relatively late in the game might not have been complete converts to the cause. After the 1980 election, Reagan interpreted his mandate broadly, offering obvious gains to business in the short run, even though thoughtful business leaders might have foreseen the problematic consequences of the proposed policies. But big business signed on anyway, because it could not afford not to.

The steel industry provides an example of the limits of business's commitment to Reaganomics. Many of the recent pronouncements of the American Iron and Steel Institute reflect basic supply side themes, but others depart from the gospel. During the 1970s, domestic steel producers, as well as other industry groups, asserted that tax rates and overregulation discouraged capital formation and investment. Government policies, they argued, tilted economic activity to favor debt (instead of equity) financing and consumption (instead of savings). Federal environmental and occupational safety and health regulations were blamed for increasing both business costs and inflation. Business executives also charged that federal economic policies and regulations were diverting capital—which was already in short supply—to areas that would not increase output per worker-hour. As the American Iron and Steel Institute put it, "These burdens of regulation . . . show up most dramatically in the collapse of productivity growth rates."[9]

The kinship between the domestic steel industry position and supply side economics ends there, however. The steel industry has used such terms as "price leadership" or "new diplomacy" to defend oligopolistic price setting, restrictions on free trade, and other practices that are anathema to pure supply side economists, whose models are based on the elimination of government interference in the market place.[10] Big business, as illustrated by the steel industry positions, has tended to sacrifice laissez faire ideology on the altar of pragmatic considerations.

Although the steel industry supports the reduction of certain taxes and regulations, it also supports government quotas, tariffs, and other import restraints on foreign steel shipments into U.S. markets. Steel executives have fought for and won voluntary import restraint agreements and trigger pricing mechanisms that have in effect placed a government supported floor under steel prices. In addition, they have asked the government to fund a major portion of the industry's research and development. Business likes the advantages it sees in the Reagan economic program but is reluctant to give up the helping hand it received from the more interventionist economic policies of past administrations.

There were, therefore, differing degrees of business commitment to the Reagan economic program at the outset. It appears that some business representatives joined the Reagan camp as fellow travelers, without having become true believers. Nonetheless, the business community has pushed and guided many portions of the administration's key proposals through Congress. The Reagan program has offered employers an unprecedented opportunity to recoup the legislative losses of past decades.

Seizing Opportunities

The passage of the 1981 Economic Recovery Tax Act with heavy business backing showed just how much the business community stood to win by backing the supply siders. The disagreements that have occurred in its aftermath, both within the business community and between organized business and the administration, underscore the fact that many business leaders were never ideological purists when it came to Reaganomics. Moreover, business's campaign leading to the passage of the 1981 bonanza was a concerted economic offensive probably unprecedented in its scope and intensity.

During his first year in the White House, President Reagan came through with the biggest federal tax reduction in history. It included an estimated $169 billion cut in business taxes over six years and a $500 billion cut in individual taxes over the same period. From the start, the tax cut side of the Reagan plan was viewed with greater skepticism than the calls for reduction in federal spending. However, with the help of a massive lobbying effort by business interests, the administration was able to twist enough legislative arms to get the tax cuts through Congress. Corporate tax reduction had been a hot topic in the business community for years, and many of the provisions of the tax bill had originally been proposed in meetings of representatives of the major employer associations in Washington.

A united front by business lobbyists on tax policy has been a rarity. There has always been agreement on the principle that ''less is best,'' but business has been unable to agree on specific tax proposals. Uncoordinated lobbying efforts sending conflicting signals to legislators have been the rule, resulting in the defeat of many business interests.

The formation of the so-called Carlton group in 1975 represented a recognition on the part of the employer community that greater lobbying coordination would pay off. As have many such groups, it began as informal breakfast meetings to discuss congressional tax developments and business's varying tax agendas. The group eventually developed into a policy and negotiating body that hammered out a compromise depreciation schedule backed by the entire business community.

The Carlton group took its name from the Sheraton-Carlton Hotel where the tax specialists of the major business organizations breakfasted every few weeks. The regulars of the group were representatives of the NAM, the Chamber, the Business Roundtable, the National Federation of Independent Business, the American Council for Capital Formation, the Committee for Effective Capital Recovery, and the Retail Tax Committee. The American Council for Capital Formation, formed in 1973 and chaired by Charls E. Walker, the head of a business consulting firm and former deputy secretary of the Treasury, originally focused on tax and regulatory policies as they affected capital investment rates. It switched in 1978 to a campaign in support of cuts in capital gains taxes. Walker was a leading force in founding the Carlton group, and the American Council has been described as an extension of his lobbying firm, which represents many large corporations. The Committee for Effective Capital Recovery, with some 500 corporate members, was created in 1971 to 'back the business investment tax credit. The Retail Tax Committee has represented the ten largest retail companies in America since 1978. In 1980, a representative of the newly formed American Business Conference, an organization of some 100 growth companies, joined the Carlton group.

The Carlton group might have remained a loose group meeting for the purpose of exchanging information had it not been for prodding by Representatives James R. Jones of Oklahoma and Barber B. Conable, Jr., of New York. These two members of the House Ways and Means Committee told the Carlton group that they would support a bipartisan overhaul of the tax depreciation laws if the group's members would agree on a proposal. The group proposed an accelerated tax depreciation for buildings (ten years), equipment and machinery (five years), and motor vehicles (three years)—the 10–5–3 business tax write-off. The significance of this consensus should not be underestimated. As Clifford T. Massa III—a member of the Carlton group and a partner of a major Washington lobbying firm—pointed out, "The problem was that we could agree on a negative agenda when we had a common threat, but everybody's affirmative agenda was different."[11]

Employers were not originally in favor of the Kemp-Roth 30-percent cut in individual tax rates, but they demonstrated their pragmatism by agreeing to support it if the Reagan administration would agree to incorporate the 10–5–3 provision into the bill. With this agreement, the administration added some extra sweeteners to win over key votes on the tax committees. To pay for these sweeteners, the administration altered the 10–5–3 formula somewhat. When it unveiled the compromise, it found the business community up in arms. Reagan administration officials had not realized the degree to which business backing had rested on the specifics of 10–5–3. Some small business lobbyists who had never liked the Jones-Conable approach felt that their support had been taken for granted and began to make deals with the Democrats. Until then, the special interests had held off on the understanding that their needs would be met in a second tax bill. However, when Democratic leaders tried to win business support for their alternative tax package, individual business interests saw a major opportunity for additional targeted cuts.

Small business groups pushed for special treatment of business inventories, capital costs, and reductions of small business income subject to tax. Thrift institutions won special "all savers" accounts and other methods to raise funds at reduced costs. High technology companies won special tax-expenditure subsidies for research and development outlays. Distressed industries won the right to "sell" their tax credits to profitable companies. Farmers and small business got major changes in the inheritance tax system, and oil, gas, and other natural resource producers won new formulas for valuing their assets. In some cases, lawmakers switched sides several times as sweeter deals were made for their leading business constituents.[12] In the end, many individual business interests had made a killing, some—including certain small business constituencies—were disappointed, and 10–5–3 had been somewhat watered down. Buildings were given a fifteen-year write-off rather than ten. Overall, though, it was quite a package—there was something for everyone, and no one left empty-handed as the federal treasury was depleted.

Same Old Game

Though delayed, the special dealing eventually took place just as in previous congresses. In the eyes of some true believers in Reaganomics, the process of implementation sullied supply side theory. David Stockman, director of the Office of Management and Budget, showed his frustrations when he plaintively described the scene: "The hogs were really feeding. The greed level, the level of opportunism, just got out of control." He acknowledged, however: "You can't put together a majority coalition unless you are willing to deal with those marginal interests that will give you the votes needed to win. That's where it is fought—on the margins—and unless you deal with those marginal votes, you can't win." [13]

The fight over the tax bill demonstrated that the game remained essentially the same, despite a friendly majority leadership in the Senate and a new leadership in the White House dedicated to an economic theory promising a radical change in the direction of government. Conservatives had criticized liberal politicians for being overgenerous with other people's money and for a lack of ability to evaluate the claims being made on them. However, Stockman and his fellow planners, assigned to carry out the Reaganomics crusade, found to their dismay that conservatives were also unable to stick to the administration's prescribed, though generous, course. "What had changed, fundamentally," Stockman lamented, "was the list of winning clients, not the nature of the game." [14]

Stockman may have been concerned with principles and the long-run effects of the tax cuts, but the business lobbyists were playing a different game. The 1981 maneuvers over the tax and budget bills were the first major legislative offensives launched by the business community in years; the bulk of the victories claimed by business in the 1970s were defensive actions.

Playing to win—rather than playing not to lose—called for a change in tactics. In order to get the best possible tax reduction deal, the business lobbyists had to order their priorities before they presented their proposals to Congress. For the business community to reach consensus to back a bill is much more difficult than is agreement to fight against a pending measure. The final product has to have the backing of its sponsors or else they will not be willing to make the lobbying effort necessary to get it passed. The legislative operations of the business community in favor of both the tax and budget cuts were very closely coordinated with administration efforts and relied heavily on business grass-roots lobbying and media support to persuade reluctant members of Congress to climb on the bandwagon.

Needless to say, the relationship between the business community and the White House changed drastically when Reagan took office. In contrast to the Carter administration, which only used business's grass-roots organization to push specific, narrow policies through Congress, the Reagan administration relied on business lobbies to get its policies sold to the multitudes and passed by Congress. As *Fortune* put it, "Reaganauts hardly need instruction on the workings of the market or the costs of regulaton. What they do need is help in putting grass-roots pressure on Democratic Congressmen—something the Roundtable's executive-suite celebrities are ill-equipped to do." [15] As a result, the Chamber moved up a notch in 1981 on the roster of Washington business associations. When Reagan deserted pure supply side economics a year later, the top Chamber staff—including President Richard Lesher—remained true believers. The relations between the Chamber and the Reagan White House might have cooled off, but the two remained dependent upon each other.[16]

Goodbye Consensus

The breakdown of consensus on economic policy in the aftermath of the passage of the 1981 tax and budget acts demonstrates both the unevenness of the business commitment to the tenets of Reaganomics and the fragility of employer unity. It also underscores the obvious failure of Reaganomics to deliver on all its promises.

The 1981 tax cuts were sold to the public as a means to economic recovery and growth. According to supply side theorists, by placing more capital at the disposal of business and individuals, tax cuts would spur investment and lead to recovery and sustained economic growth.

The facts did not fit the rosy future promised by the White House, however. The recession, combined with high interest rates and reduced sales, forced business executives to scale back rather than boost their investment plans. Not only did the rational expectation theories regarding investment and economic growth fail to materialize as fast as supply-siders predicted, but the huge tax cuts and the recession combined to push unemployment to the highest levels seen since the 1930s and to increase the federal budget deficit to record peacetime levels. As a result, a growing number of companies and industries faced serious problems and the bankruptcy rate of business matched the levels of the Great Depression. Auto dealers, home builders, and farmers were among the major victims.

Reaganomics put business on the spot. In return for rather remarkable generosity in the 1981 tax act, business investment was supposed to produce economic growth. Francis W. Steckmast, in his report to the Business Round-table on corporate performance, recognized this when he said, "Despite their cheering in the wake of the 1980 elections, corporate executives, more than ever, are on trial to deliver results."[17]

Within six months of the passage of his program by Congress, President Reagan acknowledged the need to seek a tax boost on top of another round of budget cuts. Top business executives continued to cautiously endorse the Reagan program for the record, but their actions betrayed a lack of confidence. The Business Council predicted at the end of 1981 that capital investment would not increase at the pace anticipated by White House officials. The Business Roundtable was even blunter. Its leaders reportedly told administration officials that there would be "no more blind following" of White

House policy. As the former chief of DuPont, Irving Shapiro, explained: "Businessmen are fundamentally Republicans. They persuaded themselves to back a new Republican administration 100 percent. They did that although they had misgivings."[18]

By the spring of 1982, business leaders were voicing publicly their concerns about the growing deficit. Business leaders increasingly realized the need to alter tax policy, but could reach no agreement on how to do it. Business unity had been easy to come by in 1981 when every interest could get a slice of the pie, but when it came to increasing taxes, consensus proved unattainable. The Carlton group, which had been successful in hammering out a compromise the year before, was divided.

An inside look at a meeting of the NAM tax policy committee shows that although businessmen knew what was at stake, they didn't know what to do about it. Russell B. Milliken of Mead Corporation thought that "the issue is the public perception that corporations are not paying taxes." Others were concerned about the possibility of a political backlash. In brief, the participants in the NAM deliberations represented too many interests to be able to hammer out a consensus. Said Thomas J. McHugh, vice president of Dart and Kraft, Inc., "There aren't enough decades in the century to decide whose ox would be gored."[19]

The issue was where to raise more revenue. Among the proposals being bandied about were the imposition of a minimum corporate tax, the repeal or modification of the tax leasing provision of the 1981 act, and the repeal or delay of the third year of the individual tax cut. Most of the main employer organizations opposed the minimum corporate tax, though it was favored by the National Federation of Independent Business because its $50,000 exemption would have excluded most of its members from any liability. The Business Roundtable favored repealing the ten percent individual tax cut scheduled for July 1, 1983, though the Chamber, the NFIB, and the American Business Conference were strongly opposed. The tax leasing provision was an especially controversial issue. It was strongly supported by the Chamber and the NAM and opposed by the NFIB and the American Business Conference. The Roundtable was lukewarm because it reportedly felt that the adverse publicity surrounding the provision contributed to public sentiment that business had been truly greedy in 1981. Tax leasing was favored by the steel, auto, and airline industries because it permitted companies that were suffering seriously in the recession to sell the tax breaks they could not use. Lacking immediate consensus, a flat tax rate surfaced as an alternative to be considered at some future date.

The main business negotiators on the 1982 tax bill consisted of the Business Roundtable, the NAM, the NFIB, and the American Business Conference. Other less regular participants included the National Small Business Association, National Association of Wholesaler Distributors, and various members of the Carlton group. It is significant that the ABC moved in happily when the Chamber left a gap in the leadership. In September 1981, Lesher of the Chamber had said of the ABC, "One man, a secretary, and an answering service is just not going to make a hell of a lot of difference."[20] Lesher seems to have overlooked the value of flexibility.

The business community's involvement with tax policy in the first half of the Reagan administration's term in office points up the unevenness of its commitment to Reaganomics. In 1981, it backed the supply-siders and was handsomely rewarded for its support; in 1982, business organizations with few exceptions continued to cheer Reaganomics, but their loyalties were divided. Many business lobbyists showed greater interest in protecting the gains made by business a year earlier than in helping the president shore up his program. As President Reagan started his third year in office, a group of business leaders backed by prestigious establishment economists and others called for abandoning some of the basic tenets of Reaganomics in favor of more traditionally conservative economic policy.

Constraints on the New Order

The election of President Reagan offered the employer community its best shot in a number of years at achieving a major rollback of protective labor laws that it had considered burdensome. In the first half of the Reagan term, business was notably successful at reining in welfare outlays, but made little legislative progress on other related issues. Business lobbies had greater success in securing cooperation of appointed officials to bend regulations in favor of business. But the laws remained unchanged, enforceable by the courts or by a succeeding administration.

By placing top priority on overall economic policy, the Reagan administration had to defer action on other favored legislation. Deregulation of the workplace carried too high a political price to be implemented legislatively; administrative change appeared to offer the easy way out for the Reagan team. For example, the Davis-Bacon Act and the Walsh-Healy Act are both extremely important to organized labor. Their repeal would have galvanized even the conservative segments of the AFL-CIO and allied groups into intensifying their attacks on the administration. To justify taking on issues of this kind, the administration would have needed an outpouring of public support. The business community has demonstrated that it is capable of generating that kind of public sentiment, but it cannot do so on demand. Similarly, many members of Congress prefer to avoid highly charged issues because they invariably entail lasting liabilities. The Reagan administration apparently decided that raising one major issue at a time was all it could handle effectively.

Once business and the administration won their important tax and budget battles in 1981, they needed convincing results to justify pressing their legislative agenda. Had the economy responded to the massive supply side measures, business and its allies could have argued persuasively that the free market would do the job and that workers' protective legislation and regulation of the market place constituted unnecessary restrictions on economic growth. Given the recession, employer lobbyists could only argue that the protections were costly, but they were hard put to maintain that the protections were not needed. The electorate, in fact, has shown itself to be much in favor of specific labor and social welfare programs. When it comes to cutting specific programs, the public reaction is loud and clear in favor of welfare legislation—witness social security. A similar consensus has developed that it is the business of government to regulate workplace hazards, protect private pensions, and train the unskilled. A Roper survey found that the proportion of the population favoring cuts in welfare spending dropped from 58 percent in 1980 to 45 percent in 1983.[21]

Finally, Congressional politics placed constraints on legislating change in the nation's labor policy. The House Education and Labor Committee remained under the control of liberal Democrats. Even in the Republican-controlled Senate, moderate Republicans on the Senate Labor and Human Resources Committee occasionally voted with the Democrats, frustrating the wishes of the conservative Republican majority led by Chairman Orrin Hatch of Utah.

The business lobbies have reacted realistically to these constraints. Despite some sentiment among employers for repealing or radically modifying OSHA, ERISA, Davis-Bacon, minimum wage, and other protective labor statutes, employer organizations have tended to call for reforms and "simplifications" of such laws. They recognize repeal as strictly pie in the sky. Business has learned that public opinion sets limits on what is politically feasible, limits it can violate only at its own peril.

Business has nonetheless profited handsomely from Reagan's 1981 economic policy, although adverse conditions forced the administration to institute "give backs" next year, with the reluctant acquiescence of most business organizations. One could argue that what the government gives it can also take away, but on the whole, business came out way ahead in the first half of the Reagan term. Whether business can hang onto that advantage in the long run remains an open question. What happens if supply side economics cannot deliver on all its promises? "The fact is," political analyst David Broder noted, "that business bought in on the Reagan program in 1981 and business cannot bail out in 1982 without getting hurt."[22]

The business community may already have become too closely identified with the conservative agenda for its own political good. In the spring of 1982, a national Louis Harris survey found that only about 25 percent of the business executives sampled thought that business would be hit with a major share of the blame for poor economic results after enactment of the Reagan administration's supply side economics. However, the Harris survey of the general public at the same time indicated quite a different reaction. A majority said that given a choice between a candidate who favored more breaks for business and one who was critical of business, it would back the antibusiness candidate. In fact, it appeared that the public was blaming business for problems resulting in plant closings, unemployment, and poor productivity growth. *Business Week* editorialized: "People in business may well think that being tagged with such responsibility [for solving the nation's economic ills] is a bum rap, but they can ignore these findings only at their own peril."[23] Not surprisingly, not all business representatives necessarily agree with this assessment. Richard Rahn, chief economist of the Chamber, expressed the view that Congress has been converted to the business point of view for good. He anticipated more legislation favoring business once the recession was over. Similarly, John Albertine, president of the American Business Conference, recognized that support for probusiness legislation had weakened in Congress by 1982, but he comforted his constituents by assuring them "we are still a long way away from 1975."[24]

Beyond Cupidity?

Despite the vast wealth and market power concentrated in the hands of the business elite, it is clear that it does not have an unrivaled control in politics. Despite the employer community's remarkable grass-roots organization, PAC war chests supporting candidates in both parties, and research resources, business lobbies, even when they agree, still must work at fostering coalitions to push even their common legislative goals.

Adam Smith is quoted frequently as the champion of the free market, but only half of Smith's story is usually told. The originator of the invisible hand was also concerned that the free enterprise system could founder on avarice. Smith's self-interest was one that was harnessed by diverse and competing economic, political, and social forces that would promote the general welfare. His vision moved beyond individual greed to include a system or philosophy of "natural liberty" in which all segments of society benefited and wealth replaced poverty. Freedom and a chance at self-actualization were not to be confined to a select few.

For the business community to remain on top in Washington will require a social vision rivaling that of Adam Smith. Unchecked pursuit of narrow self-interest is not enough. If the public is persuaded that tax reductions and rapid depreciation of business investments are not enhancing capital invest- ments that generate jobs and raise productivity, then the business community can expect to fall from grace. If the new incentives granted business result in greater maldistribution of income and wealth, then the changes instituted under the banner of supply side economics may be short-lived.

Thoughtful business leaders have expressed genuine hope that this will not happen. As one business executive, a former president of the Ford Motor Company and dean of the Stanford University business school, put it:

> If business mistakenly believes that the clock can be turned back, it
> will fail to make significant gains that are possible in the current
> environment. . . . By placing too great reliance on an ideology that
> will not work in its simplest form, the resulting disillusionment will
> lead to an early reversal of the current pro-business climate.[25]

It remains the task of the business community to transform the largess be- stowed by Reaganomics upon it into gains experienced by the rest of society. If business fails to do so, the 1981 gains may turn out to be an ephemeral victory that will be unlikely to recur for years to come.

II

It Pays to Do Homework

A Formidable Team

The business community lobbies and their support organizations, including think tanks, constitute a rather formidable and wide-ranging establishment. They are tremendously diverse, have enormous resources on which to draw, and have been able to pool their assets in ways that have had quite substantial legislative payoffs. Employers and their allies have achieved a notable degree of unity and cooperation on a number of key economic, social welfare, and labor policy issues over the past decade. One of the most important ways of overcoming the diversity within their ranks has been to build coalitions to pursue specific legislative goals. They initially learned to close ranks when fighting defensive battles; more recently they have taken to the attack in order to reverse unwelcome governmental intervention.

The intent of the business organizations so far has not been to jettison the welfare state or destroy the social progress made in the 1960s and 1970s. They have recognized the utility of keeping the shell of the welfare state while doing away with what the business community considers "excesses." There is, however, little agreement on the proper limits of the welfare state. Even though business organizations have made progress in presenting a united front in Washington, they do not necessarily speak with one voice on all issues. In fact, quite frequently one business interest will welcome what another group considers unwarranted governmental intervention. The following three case studies—dealing with private pensions, unemployment benefits, and labor law—demonstrate that a call to arms may still find business groups marching in different directions.

5

Private Pension Issues: Locking the Barn after the Horse Has Been Stolen

On Labor Day 1974, President Gerald Ford signed the Employee Retirement Income Security Act (ERISA), a law affecting almost every major corporation in the United States, many smaller employers, and a large proportion of their employees. The law regulates the most important investment source in the country and establishes the pension rights of active and retired workers and their employers. On signing the bill, President Ford said that the legislation would "probably give more benefits and rights and success in the area of labor-management than almost anything in the history of the country."[1]

Although President Ford's hyperbole was routine for such an occasion, few would dispute that the bill he signed was of major importance. It is surprising, therefore, that the employer community did not fully anticipate the federal regulation of private pensions. Holding fast to the view that pensions were within the preserve of managerial prerogative, business organizations were late in appraising the proposed legislation. By failing to offer acceptable alternatives, business exercised only modest influence on the law's content. Though pension regulation had been discussed in and out of Congress since the late 1950s and the first comprehensive bill had been introduced in 1967, business representatives were remarkably unprepared for its passage.

By the time the major employer organizations mobilized their resources for a serious fight against the proposed pension legislation, the Senate Committee on Labor and Public Welfare had already reported out a bill. The business lobbyists' failure to make a positive contribution to the law's provisions reflected not only a gap in their political intelligence, but more significantly the lack of pension expertise among top management. This lack led to an underestimation of the potential cost of ERISA. As one Chamber of Commerce staff member recalled, discussion of the pension issue with business executives led to glazed eyes and a quick change of subject.

Employer organizations participated in the policy debate and tended to share a similar perspective, though they disagreed on many of the details. Their active lobbying against proposed pension regulation began in the early 1970s, but there was relatively little coordination among the organizations until it was too late. Overall, there was a gradual process of accommodation on the part of the business community, with employer representatives compromising on nearly all major issues. Business might have been more successful had its alternatives to liberal policy been more acceptable and uniform. The interests of small employers were poorly represented in the deliberations and, as a result, the provisions of the law reflected some disregard for their needs.

Following the passage of ERISA, big business set up an organization to represent its views on private pension issues. To strengthen their hand, large employers have rallied to the side of small employers in an effort to ''simplify'' ERISA by cutting down on paperwork and, incidentally, on employee protections. Employers have found it difficult, however, to undo what was done in 1974. Having granted the principle of federal regulation of private pension plans in the ERISA battle, business lobbyists have had their hands full preventing further encroachments, or even controlling the agenda for public debate. For example, the business community had hoped that the President's Commission on Pension Policy established in 1978 would deal with issues of ERISA's alleged overregulation; instead, the commission recommended far-reaching governmental intervention. The political climate is more favorable now to a rollback of ERISA's excesses (as employers would have it), but employers are still finding it an uphill struggle to amend the act. Their efforts have been stymied thus far by the inertia of the status quo, problems of differing priorities within their own ranks, and vocal representation of retirees' interests.

In the eight years since ERISA's passage, the only major amendment has been the Multiemployer Pension Plan Amendments Act of 1980. This law contains advantageous provisions for some multiemployer pension plan sponsors but vastly increases ERISA's costs to many others. Congress acted to prevent the collapse of the multiemployer plan termination insurance system only when segments of organized business and labor agreed on the proposals. Business support for the 1980 act has dissipated in the wake of its passage, however. Calls for its revision have demonstrated graphically the fragility of employer unity as well as the difficulty of regaining lost ground.

The Stakes and the Players

Federal policy on private pensions has always sparked tremendous controversy because the stakes are so high for the interested parties. The main issues that concern employers relate to the cost of private pension plans and their control.

Pensions provided by employers to take care of workers in their retirement are a relatively recent phenomenon. The first plan was established by the American Express Company in 1875. Many plans that were established prior to the 1930s did not survive the Great Depression, and unions as well as employers turned to the federal government to provide retirement income. The result was the Social Security Act of 1935.

Private pensions grew considerably during the Second World War when government policy favored deferred payments to employees in order to relieve inflationary pressures. The growth of pension plans was further accelerated following a strike by the Steelworkers Union over pensions and by the 1949 Supreme Court action in *Inland Steel Co. v. NLRB,* which upheld a lower court ruling that pensions are deferred wages and therefore a subject for collective bargaining under the National Labor Relations Act. Half of the work force is now covered by private pensions, and the number of beneficiaries had risen to over seven million in 1975. Investments in private pensions rose from $12 billion in 1950 to an estimated $600 billion three decades later.

Although humanitarian motives have no doubt played a role in inducing management to provide private pensions for employees, sound management considerations should not be ignored. The earliest plans were established without collective bargaining, and payment was entirely discretionary for the employer. Pensions provided a means of industrial discipline and tended to reduce labor turnover, thereby reducing search and training costs for new workers.[2] Pensions also offered employers a socially acceptable means of easing older, less productive employees out of their jobs.[3]

Employers have in addition a very important interest in pensions as tax shelters. Beginning in the 1920s—and particularly since enactment of the Internal Revenue Act of 1942—the government has offered employers considerable incentives to establish qualified pension plans. Tax liabilities are reduced when a company establishes a pension plan. In 1982, the estimated federal revenue loss due to pension contributions and earnings amounted to $45 billion. Employer plans and plans for the self-employed accounted for another $2.8 billion in tax expenditures.[4]

Finally, pension funds represent the largest single pool of new investment capital. American companies and the financial community have a tremendous interest in maintaining control over these vast funds. Though ERISA imposes restrictions on how those funds might be used, there is still considerable latitude for plan sponsors and pension fund trustees to use the funds in ways to improve their profit and market positions.

Of course, the pension industry has had a vested interest in the existing pension system. The Association of Private Pension and Welfare Plans was perhaps the most active representative of big business in the ERISA battle. Formed in 1967 to meet the threat of federal pension standards, its members include pension consultants, attorneys, accounting firms, investment houses, insurance companies, collectively bargained pension funds, and employers. The American Society of Pension Actuaries, whose members service small firms, has tended to reflect the small employer's concerns.

The American Bankers Association, whose members act as trustees for numerous pension funds, also has a strong stake in pension plans and their regulation, particularly fiduciary standards. The banking and pension industries initially opposed most of ERISA's provisions, as did their clients, though both industries stood to benefit from what was to be a complex law requiring expert consulting services that only they could provide. The life insurance industry, which provides the funding arrangements for many pension plans, is another important group involved in pension administration and regulation.

In addition to the industry groups, there was representation for active workers and retirees. The United Steelworkers of America and the United Automobile Workers were out in front, with other unions also actively involved. Retirees were represented by Ralph Nader's Public Interest Research Group, as well as by retiree groups. These vast constituencies, each directly affected by national pension policy, have been playing—and continue to play—for enormously high stakes.

The Long Road to ERISA

ERISA was preceded by the Welfare and Pension Plan Disclosure Act of 1958, which required plan administrators to file annual reports on the structure and operation of pension funds. Congress passed the disclosure law in response to hearings that disclosed corruption and mishandling of pension funds by their trustees. The worst cases involved multiemployer plans.

Employers generally opposed governmental intervention in pension plan administration, but for various reasons. Representatives of employers with single and multiemployer plans emphasized different arguments.[5] The debate over regulating pension plans in the late 1960s and early 1970s elicited a repeat performance by employer organizations. The issues involved in ERISA were, however, more complex and the stakes much greater than they had been in the disclosure controversy.

ERISA had its origins in complaints from participants in private pension plans. The termination by Studebaker-Packard Corporation of its pension plan in 1964 generated interest in government regulation of private pension plans. A cabinet-level committee appointed by President Johnson in 1965 to review federal policy toward retirement programs recommended (without presidential endorsement) minimum federal standards for funding pension plans and maximum age and service requirements for individuals to vest in (qualify for) such plans. It did not recommend enactment of a new statute setting standards, but favored regulating private pension plans through the tax code. These recommendations received mixed reviews from the President's Advisory Committee on Labor-Management Policy, which favored more adequate funding of pension plans but rejected the proposal requiring vesting rules as a condition for favorable tax treatment. The advisory committee held that such a requirement might "unduly burden" the administration of existing plans or hamper the establishment of new ones. This position would be echoed many times by employer representatives testifying before congressional committees, though the labor movement would later support such federal standards.

The first comprehensive reform bill was introduced in 1967, but seven years elapsed before ERISA's passage. There were a number of reasons for the act's long gestation; foremost was the tremendous complexity of the issues.[6] Both the House and Senate established special task forces to study the costs and benefits of various legislative proposals. Had employers been more active at this stage, they might have been more successful later on in influencing the legislation. The work involved the labor and tax writing committees of both houses, whose interest in pensions reflected different philosophical perspectives: the labor committees were more concerned with the human dimension, and the tax committees focused on the fiscal consequences of any new law.

The Nixon administration's initial proposal to tighten standards for trustees of pension funds and to require greater disclosure by pension plan sponsors never got out of committee because the members wanted broader legislation. In late 1971, responding to pressure from the White House Conference on Aging, the administration endorsed modified standards for funding plans and vesting but opposed portability of pension rights and plan termination insurance. It also proposed changes in the tax laws to encourage self-employed persons and individuals without pension coverage to save for their own retirement. This essentially remained the administration's position throughout the debate, but the Watergate scandals prevented the Nixon administration from impressing its view on Congress.

Senator Jacob Javits of New York, the ranking minority member of the Senate Labor and Public Welfare Committee, was the leader in pressing for pension legislation. He had introduced his first pension bill in 1967. Four years elapsed before the Senate Labor Subcommittee, chaired by Senator Harrison Williams of New Jersey, undertook a series of well-publicized hearings highlighting pension plan abuses. Many witnesses at these hearings had lost pension benefits they had expected to receive. Williams and Javits skillfully used these hearings to generate public interest in the problem. Business representatives complained that the committee publicized exceptional cases that should not be used as the basis for legislation. But the parade of horror stories swayed public opinion in favor of a comprehensive bill, making outright opposition an untenable position.

When Williams (who also chaired the full Senate committee) and Javits agreed on the terms for a joint bill, the chances for ERISA's enactment were vastly improved. A bill was reported out of the Labor Committee in late 1972, but was not voted on by the full Senate until the next year. By the time the House Labor Subcommittee turned its attention to the bill, it was too late for the employers' views to prevail.

The product of this long debate was an act that set a variety of significant federal standards safeguarding the pension rights of active workers and retirees and spelled out the obligations of plan sponsors and trustees. The act also regulated the tax status of pension funds. In brief, ERISA imposed tougher reporting and disclosure standards than did the 1958 act and set minimum standards for the action of fiduciaries charged with the management of pension fund assets. The law established rules governing eligibility and vesting rights in terms of an employee's age and years of consecutive service with the employer. Workers were vested in a pension (or a portion thereof) based on their age and years of service whether or not they continued to work for the sponsoring company until retirement. The act also established individual retirement accounts (IRAs), which give individuals incentives to save for their own retirement and provide a vehicle for the limited portability of pension benefits when employees change jobs. The heart of the bill was the minimum funding standards for pension plans and the plan termination insurance program, which guaranteed the payment of pension benefits to beneficiaries of defined benefit plans in the event of a fund's bankruptcy. The most controversial provisions of ERISA were those concerning vesting and funding standards and the termination insurance program. ERISA's provisions (excepting termination insurance) applied both to defined benefit plans, which obligate the employer to pay a worker on retirement a fixed dollar amount or a percentage of the employee's pay, and defined contribution plans, which obligate the employer to contribute a specified amount to a retirement fund each month and which entitle the worker on retirement to the accumulated funds plus interest.

The ERISA Debate: Gradual Compromise

Because of the novelty of the ERISA approach, the breadth of its regulation of private plans, and the size of the stakes for all parties, it was a highly controversial statute and engendered a lively and lengthy public debate. Employers' priorities differed according to the scope and type of the plan they sponsored, and this affected their preferred compromise positions. Nevertheless, for the most part there was an identifiable employer position throughout the ERISA debate.

Stripped of the high-sounding rhetoric, the core of the debate was money. Advocates favored federal standards aimed at protecting employees' pensions, and employers opposed federal intervention because it would involve added costs. Since Congress set out to promulgate standards for pension plans but not to mandate such plans, there was concern throughout the deliberations that standards imposing substantial cost increases could result in fewer plans and thus prove self-defeating. A related employer theme was the need for flexibility in pension plan administration. Employers were almost as concerned about losing control over their pension plans as about cost, though the two were clearly closely linked.

In addition to opposing ERISA for reasons of cost and control, some employer representatives also addressed the reformers' arguments directly. For the most part, business was unable to offer alternatives that would have adequately addressed the problems faced by the pension system. However, the arguments marshaled against the portability proposals did, in the end, carry the day. Some of the criticisms of the plan termination insurance program have proven to be true since the law's passage, though their validity was not accepted at the time. Trying to shape the requirements to minimize the costs of reporting, disclosure, and fiduciary standards, the employers compromised early. The compromises involving vesting and minimum funding were harder to reach, for here federal standards were potentially the most costly. The standards legislated tended to adopt the practices of the large companies, placing in some cases an undue burden upon those employers who were poorly represented in the deliberations.

The employers' strategy in the ERISA battle reflected a gradual learning process concerning what positions were feasible in light of political realities. Generally, management played its traditional nay-saying role until the early 1970s. At that point the larger associations, sensing that Congress was moving toward some form of legislation, began to edge away from their earlier ideological stances. In 1970 and 1971, the leading employer organizations limited their support to modest changes in the areas of fiduciary responsibility and reporting and disclosure. In 1972, they made a major turnabout in accepting some form of compulsory vesting standards. Under pressure from both Congress and the administration, further compromise was made in 1973 on funding standards.

The changing attitudes of employer organizations were reflected in an internal NAM memorandum, dated May 17, 1972, addressed to the board of

directors by the organization's employee benefits committee. The writer
recognized, albeit belatedly, the futility of the NAM's rigid approach to
pension legislation.

> Outright and total opposition to all [broad reform] places us in an
> inflexible and tenuous position similar to the one NAM experienced
> during the legislative battle on occupational safety and health [in
> 1970]. . . . There is every indication that legislation on private
> pension plans is imminent. The only question that remains is what
> kind of legislation.[7]

Coverage

Pension law reformers sought to broaden pension coverage by reducing
requirements for vesting, easing rules governing participation, and removing
obstacles to pension portability. Of these, vesting received the most attention.

Before ERISA, vesting provisions varied widely. Some plans had no vesting
provisions, entitling employees to a pension only upon retirement. A number of
proposals were put forward to address this issue. Employer representatives
were united in their initial opposition to any minimum vesting standards and
could not agree on a preferred formula when it became clear that a vesting
provision was inevitable. The business argument was that increasing costs
risked slowing the growth of private pension plans and even reducing benefits
to workers. There was also concern about leaving employers enough flexibility
to accommodate the competing needs of workers of differing status and age
groups. A more basic argument claimed that vesting standards in the majority
of private plans were adequate and if there had to be legislation for minimum
standards, care should be taken not to exceed existing costs.

Employer representatives failed to stress the trade-off between having more
plans with stringent vesting requirements that would sharply limit entitlement
to pensions and fewer plans from which more employees would ultimately
benefit. Being covered by a pension plan was not much good to the employee
who was unable to meet the, say, twenty-five year service requirement for
vesting. The NAM and the national Chamber initially opposed compulsory
vesting, but by mid-1972 had come around to supporting 100 percent vesting
after ten years because it was already in many plans. In June 1972, the Chamber
announced its support for "reasonable federal standards or regulation governing vesting of private pensions."[8] The two main business organizations tended
to reflect a big business bias on the vesting issue. Small employers held out for
fewer restrictive standards. The National Retail Merchants Association conceded that if a standard had to be legislated, it should start with 50 percent

vesting after fifteen years and should increase by 10 percent each year, with full vesting after twenty years.[9]

As finally enacted, the law provided three options: (1) full vesting after ten years; (2) a "rule of forty-five," which entitled the employee to 50 percent vesting when his or her age and service totaled forty-five, with a subsequent increase of 10 percent annually; and (3) "graded vesting," which qualified an employee for a partial pension after a predetermined duration of service, with the vesting gradually increasing to 100 percent after fifteen years of service. The vesting provisions were among the more costly features of the law and have contributed to the termination of some plans since 1974.

Employers also sought to reduce costs through the enactment of stringent standards for participation. The Chamber, for example, favored requiring that an employee be at least thirty years of age and have worked three years in order to qualify for participation in a plan. The business community did not stage its big battle over participation standards, however, because the payout of benefits is more directly related to conditions for vesting. Since liberal vesting standards were potentially more costly than liberal participation standards, employers saved their bargaining for the vesting battle. The participation standard eventually enacted was, in fact, quite liberal—twenty-five years of age with one year of service.

A third issue involved the institution of a portability system whereby a worker's pension rights earned at one company would be honored by succeeding employers. Employers argued that any portability system would not only prevent companies from using pensions to attract or retain personnel, but would also raise costs, which remain low because many workers quit their jobs before they accumulate pension rights.

Any portability scheme—whether it involved the establishment of a central portability fund for private pension credits or the mandatory portability of pension credits from one employer's plan to another—would have increased costs appreciably. The technical problems also loomed large and would have increased the role of public decisionmaking in private pensions. Universal portability could be more efficiently achieved through the social security system. The arguments against portability were persuasive, and support never materialized for any one mandatory portability scheme. The law made no provision for mandatory portability but encouraged individual retirement accounts by allowing tax-deferred savings. These provisions were strengthened by the 1981 tax law changes.

Financial Protections

The most important concern of ERISA proponents was to assure pension plan participants of the receipt of their pensions (once vested) by preventing inadequate funding practices and insuring against the possibility of plan termination. Reformers pushed for a minimum funding standard because the internal revenue code did not set stringent funding standards. As a result of that omission, some pension funds had accumulated large unfunded liabilities and in some cases had failed to meet their obligations to retirees.

The employers' argument—that the vast majority of plans were sufficiently capitalized and adequately regulated by tax legislation and the established standards of the accounting profession[10]—was effectively challenged by advocates of the legislation.[11] Employers also argued that the costs imposed by legislating minimum standards to curb the irresponsible funding practices of the minority of employers would seriously hamper the growth of private plans. However, employers failed to rebut the argument that a pension plan unable to meet its obligations to participants was worse than no pension plan at all.

When the passage of pension regulation became imminent, employer organizations decided to compromise. Acknowledging in August 1973 that "a few plans have not been properly funded," the NAM agreed on the need for a "reasonable and flexible" funding rule. In October, the Chamber came out in favor of funding standards, including a forty-year amortization provision for past service costs and a special provision for "economic hardship cases."[12] The enacted standards required that the normal costs of administering a plan be currently funded and that the past service commitments of plans be amortized over thirty years (forty years for plans already in effect and for multiemployer plans).

The federal reinsurance proposal provoked the most vehement employer opposition. It was also one of the few issues that led to a labor-management confrontation. The unions came out strongly in favor of a government-operated insurance plan which would finance deficits resulting from plan terminations. The Studebaker case was cited as evidence that plans of even major corporations could be terminated before they were fully funded.

Employers, however, were united in their opposition to the idea. Even the Business Roundtable, which supported most ERISA provisions, objected strongly to plan termination insurance. Business voiced four major objections to the proposal.

First, employers argued that there was no strongly demonstrated need for pension insurance because terminations were rare and affected relatively few workers. The social value of protecting this small number of employees was offset by the costs the insurance program would impose, business argued. Employers were concerned not just with the direct costs of insurance premiums and the administrative burdens they entailed, but also with the impact of the employer liability provision on companies' ability to get credit, particularly in the case of small employers. Since ERISA's passage, the employers' cost predictions have been shown to have been more accurate than those of the program's proponents. Nevertheless, based on actual experience, advocates of the insurance provisions argue that the benefits still outweigh the costs.

Second, business argued that federal reinsurance of pension plans might encourage terminations because some of the risks being insured against were largely within the control of employers. This has proven to be an important structural defect in the program. Business also argued that termination insurance would distort collective bargaining and lead to overly optimistic assumptions being made at the bargaining table. It is unclear to what degree this has occurred.

Third, employers advanced the concern that a workable insurance scheme would involve the federal government in detailed control over the actuarial assumptions, financial practices, and other aspects of the operations of the funds. Experience has not borne out this predicted loss of freedom by administrators of financially solvent plans.

Finally, the insurance program was viewed as inequitable because it would require companies with relatively well funded plans to support poorly managed plans. Of course, employers as a group have never been keen on socializing the costs of doing business.

Despite its strong opposition to plan termination insurance, the national Chamber decided to compromise at the eleventh hour when it recognized that a termination insurance provision was certain to be included in ERISA. Looking for a way to minimize government's role in private pensions, the Chamber urged the congressional conferees in March 1974 to support a "non-governmental corporation" to administer the program. However, organized labor was strongly opposed to a privately managed insurance program and the insurance industry, which had tried earlier to design a privately run program, had been unable to come up with a proposal acceptable to the broad range of business interests. As a result, the Pension Benefit Guaranty Corporation was born.

Placed in the Department of Labor, the PBGC guarantees the payment of pension benefits (up to a limit) to participants in defined benefit plans in the event of a fund's inability to pay, sets insurance premiums to be paid by most plan sponsors, and makes employers liable for up to 30 percent of their net worth for benefits paid out under the insurance in the event of plan termination.

Employer Strategy

With the wisdom of hindsight, it appears that employers might have gotten pension legislation more to their liking had they been able to better coordinate their campaigns and to offer more acceptable alternatives. Clearly, they were slow to rally to the fight in earnest. The Council on Employee Benefits spoke for those large corporate employers with collectively bargained plans, and the Ad Hoc Corporate Pension Fund Committee (also known as the Washington Group on Pensions) was formed to coordinate the testimony and lobby on behalf of its forty big business members. The NAM tended to reflect big business's concerns, as did the Chamber to a slightly lesser degree. The Chamber was not nearly as responsive to the needs of its substantial small employer membership before ERISA's passage as it has been since, though it did champion tax incentives for the self-employed, a major small business concern. The lobbying by individual corporations seems to have pushed the Chamber and the NAM to compromise, perhaps faster than they would have moved in the absence of other representation. The Chamber's strategy to hold out as long as possible on key issues was undercut by the larger companies' privately expressed willingness to "live with" certain standards.

Prior to 1972, the major business organizations confined their activity mainly to intelligence gathering on the Hill and presentations of formal testimony before congressional committees, doing little lobbying for alternative approaches. However, once the Labor and Public Welfare Committee reported out its omnibus bill for a vote by the Senate, employer lobbyists stepped up their efforts. The Chamber concentrated its activities on placing the administration of the pending legislation under the jurisdiction of the Treasury rather than the Department of Labor. The employers reasoned that, since the main concern of the Treasury is with financial matters, it would be more sympathetic to the business perspective than would the Department of Labor, which they perceived as being dominated by organized labor. Senator Javits originally favored establishing an independent agency but deferred on that point to Senator Williams, who favored Labor Department jurisdiction over the entire legislation. To shift enforcement responsibility from Labor to the Treasury, the Chamber urged the Senate Finance Committee to assert jurisdiction over the proposal. The Chamber's strategy was successful, and when the legislation was reported out of the Finance Committee in late 1972, it had been stripped of all its main provisions, leaving only the disclosure and fiduciary standards. By this time, it was too late for the full Senate to consider the bill, so the matter was put off until the next year.

The Chamber victory was, however, short-lived. It succeeded in delaying action in the Ninety-second Congress. The next year, in 1973, a "gentlemen's agreement" was reached between Finance Committee Chairman Russell Long and Labor Committee Chairman Williams which achieved a jurisdictional compromise. The Finance Committee agreed not to seek jurisdiction, and the Labor Committee agreed not to seek floor action on the bill until after the Finance Committee had made its recommendations.[13]

In the fall of 1973, the business groups found, to their dismay, that the House Committee on Education and Labor bill was in many ways more attractive than the Senate-passed bill, which had been an amalgam of the bills of the Labor and Finance Committees. Though the House bill gave the Labor Department complete responsibility for enforcement and the Senate-passed bill divided jurisdiction between the Labor and Treasury departments, employers found the Senate bill's reporting provisions far more burdensome and were particularly upset about a "sleeper" provision that set a ceiling of $75,000 on retirement benefits that a corporation could pay an individual out of tax-free contributions. This provision touched high-paid business executives and incorporated professional establishments particularly, and the Chamber made its elimination a top priority.

The House Committee on Education and Labor reported out its bill in September 1973. Meanwhile, the Ways and Means Committee considered both the House Labor Committee bill and the Senate-passed bill and decided to draft its own version. In late November, the House leadership decided to put off final action on pension reform until the second session of the Ninety-third Congress. The business community was quite pleased with the delay and cranked up its grass-roots organization in a last-chance effort to make the legislation more palatable.

The employer lobbyists' most important victory in the House was modifying the limit on pension benefits financed out of tax-deductible contributions. In the Ways and Means Committee, business won two improvements. Provision was made for cost-of-living increases in the $75,000 ceiling and for a "grandfather" clause. By making an issue out of this provision, the Chamber reinforced its image of representing special interests and thereby weakened its effectiveness. Other employer groups felt that the Chamber gave too much attention to this subject, which should have been peripheral to the main issues of the ERISA debate.

Through their last-ditch attempt to influence the final shape of the legislation, the business lobbyists won a number of minor victories. First, the conference committee decided to retain the higher House limit on pension benefits from tax-deductible contributions. Second, the conference selected the House vesting provision, which offered three alternatives, over the Senate version, which provided only one. Third, employer representatives persuaded the conferees to strike the Senate's provision for a voluntary portability scheme administered by the PBGC and delayed the effective dates for compliance with ERISA standards for plans already in existence when the act was passed.

Employers were less successful in other areas. The conference committee decided on the Senate's slightly less generous tax deduction for contributions to IRAs. Business was also unhappy with the compromise arrangements that gave the Labor and Treasury Departments dual jurisdiction over vesting, participation, funding, and fiduciary standards. This arrangement would later cause serious administrative difficulties. Finally, the business community was unable to make the plan termination insurance program the responsibility of a private, nongovernmental corporation.

In light of the protracted debate, the final vote on ERISA was a veritable lovefest, attesting to the popularity of the legislation. The 1974 House vote on HR2 was 376 to 4, and the 1973 vote on HR4200 in the Senate was 93 to 0. Faced with this legislative consensus, employers had no choice but to give in on the main issues. Though business was slow to realize that ERISA was an idea whose time had come, its gradual compromise on the key policy questions— except portability and plan termination insurance—reflected its belated recognition of the need to come to grips with political reality.

To summarize, the employer lobbies succeeded in reducing the financial burdens imposed by the act. But in winning a few skirmishes, they lost the war. Conceding defeat and anticipating "an administrative and technical nightmare," Chamber spokesman Andrew Melgard found the law to be "a mixed bag." He cited as one of its beneficial aspects "a clear national policy encouraging all working persons in the private sector to save for their retirement."[14] By giving individuals such incentives, the government was indirectly relieving the pressure on employers to provide pensions for their employees. The Chamber, in its newsletter, commented about ERISA: "On balance . . . the grave danger looms that the politicians and bureaucrats have gone further than was necessary in the public interest, that they have given to themselves more control and denied to the public more freedom, than was needed to curb or cure the limited number of pension abuses that existed."[15] This guardedly pessimistic view was shared by many other business associations.

Business's Post-ERISA Predicament

The employer community was slow to face up to ERISA before 1974, but since then it has paid close attention to private pension issues in the hope of rolling back some of ERISA's more objectionable provisions. In the years since the passage of the law, business has found major obstacles to winning back what it let slip away in 1974. It took the combined support of organized labor and employer organizations to pass the Multiemployer Pension Plan Act of 1980, the only direct amendment to ERISA thus far.

Even with a profoundly conservative administration and sympathetic Senate leadership, employers have found that retaking lost ground is a most difficult task. In pension policy, the political center has not shifted back quite as far as some employers would like. Still, business claims to have won considerable support for loosening fiduciary standards, reducing reporting and disclosure requirements, and making changes in the single employer plan termination insurance program. Momentum has slowed because of conflicting priorities within the employer community, the strength of the opposition, a crowded legislative calendar on Capitol Hill, and the sheer complexity of the issues to be resolved.

Employers have not significantly changed the tune they were singing in the pre-ERISA debate. They have argued that ERISA went too far and have sought to amend it by exempting specific industries from the provisions of the law and rolling back many of its standards. Big business' interests on private pension issues are represented by the ERISA Industry Committee (ERIC), which grew out of the Washington Business Group on Pensions. It had its first meeting in October 1974 just after the act was signed, with the initial task of assuring business input to the drafting of the regulations needed to implement the law. Today, ERIC represents approximately 100 of the largest manufacturers, retailers, utilities, banks, and insurance companies and involves directly their top executives in the fields of employee benefits and labor relations. Though there are no formal ties between ERIC and the Business Roundtable, they are generally thought to represent the same segment of the business community and to cooperate informally with each other.

Since ERISA's passage, there has been increased cooperation and coordination of activities within the employer community, particularly the pension, banking, and insurance industries. The "core group" of interested employer and service provider organizations in Washington includes the Chamber, the NAM, ERIC, the Association of Private Pension and Welfare Plans, the American Society of Pension Actuaries, the American Academy of Actuaries, the American Bankers Association, and the American Council of Life Insurance. Representatives of these organizations meet periodically to exchange information and coordinate approaches to pension-related legislative proposals.

The small employer lobbies represented by the National Small Business Association and the National Federation of Independent Business have indicated increasing interest in the administration of ERISA and its future direction. Their increased activity reflects the fact that the brunt of ERISA's impact has been borne by small business; about 97 percent of all single employer plan terminations in 1975–78 have been plans with under a hundred participants. A 1981 NFIB membership survey found that about 15 percent of its members sponsor plans. Representatives of the larger employers who lobby for ERISA reforms in hopes of benefiting themselves are also helping the "smalls" in the process.

The protections ERISA has provided have not been without significant costs. The direct costs have included the dollars spent on reporting and disclosure activities, pension benefits for an expanded number of plan participants, faster funding schedules, and insurance premiums; the indirect costs have involved bypassed investment opportunities resulting from ERISA's restrictions on fiduciaries.

Of course, ERISA has created some problems (especially for small business) and needs some fine tuning. The termination insurance program has been particularly troublesome. Its problems stem mostly from the deterioration of the economy since 1974, but faulty design of the legislation must also bear part of the blame.

President's Commission on Pension Policy: Trying to Lock Up

The experience of the President's Commission on Pension Policy, established in 1978, illustrates the difficulty employers had in preventing the broadening of federal regulation of private pensions once the principle had been accepted. The commission's primary recommendation was for a mandatory universal pension system. Had the 1980 election not been a Republican landslide, mandatory pensions might have been a legislative worry for Washington's employer representatives.

The purpose of the commission was to take an overall view of private retirement policy. The idea got a mixed reception from the business community. On the one hand, employer organizations saw the commission as a possible vehicle for pinpointing and documenting some of ERISA's "excesses." On the other, they were leery of a Democratic-appointed commission. Business was, in fact, relatively well represented. The commission chairman was Peter McColough, chief executive officer of Xerox Corporation, and other members included William Greenough, then chairman of the CED Subcommittee on Retirement Policy and the former head of the nation's largest private pension fund. Ultimately, though, employers were disappointed with the commission's lack of attention to problems of cost.

The commission focused on coverage. In 1979, only 45 percent of all private sector workers were participants in a plan and only 26 percent were vested. Among the uncovered was a disproportionately large number of women and minorities. The main reasons for the lack of pension coverage were found to be high labor mobility, interrupted work patterns, absence of union representation, and employment by small employers.[16] The commission considered a number of policies to close the coverage gap, focusing on a mandatory universal pension system (MUPS).

As proposed by the commission, the system would be funded by a minimum employer contribution of 3 percent of payroll to cover all employees over the age of twenty-five with one year of service. Benefits would be fully portable, would not be integrated with social security, and vesting would be immediate. The MUPS proposal was aimed at protecting uncovered workers as well as those covered workers who could not meet ERISA's minimum vesting requirements. The commission recommended a three-year phase-in period and a special tax credit to mitigate the costs for small business. Employers could maintain the funds in pension trusts, in accounts with insurance companies, or in a central MUPS portability fund.[17]

Needless to say the employer lobbyists were unanimous in opposing the idea. Their strategy demonstrated a much greater sophistication than that displayed by business representatives in the pre-ERISA debate. Drawing on the research of the Employee Benefit Research Institute—a research group established in 1978 by the pension industry and plan sponsors—they challenged the commission's coverage estimates and emphasized tax incentives to encourage saving as an alternative to a compulsory pension system. In addition, the employer representatives favored reducing ERISA's paperwork burdens, and increasing employment opportunities for the elderly.[18] The commission's findings have been all but ignored by the Reagan administration and Congress.

The Multiemployer Problem

ERISA was designed mainly with single employer pension plans in mind. Most private pension plans cover workers at a single firm or plant, but in industries with many smaller employers, such as the needle trades, construction, and trucking, it is more common that a group of employers in a given area contributes to a plan covering all workers under the terms of a collective agreement. Though multiemployer plans account for only two percent of all pension plans, they cover almost 25 percent of total plan participants.

Acknowledging the diversity of its membership, the Chamber took the easy way out, favoring the same treatment for single and multiemployer plans. However, trade associations (such as the Associated General Contractors) and some unions actively called for exemptions from various provisions for multiemployer plans. They argued for exemption from the vesting standard on the ground that workers in multiemployer plans already enjoyed a degree of vesting not found in single employer plans, since they frequently changed jobs among the sponsoring firms with no loss of pension rights. Opponents pointed out, however, that single employer plans of major corporations offered the same kind of portability among their plants and offices nationwide. The multiemployer argument against funding standards and termination insurance was that multiemployer plans, being based on coinsurance principles, were inherently financially more stable than single employer plans. This financial stability premise would be called into question after ERISA's passage, though not before.

The multiemployer argument did not prevail in the vesting debate, though unions and employers with multiemployer plans did win other concessions. These included ten additional years for basic funding of past service liabilities, a separate termination insurance fund for multiemployer plans, a lower premium rate, and a delay in the effective date of mandatory coverage of multiemployer plans under the termination insurance program.

The Multiemployer Pension Plan Amendments Act of 1980 restructured the multiemployer plan termination insurance program so as to avoid potentially costly problems arising from changed economic circumstances since 1974 and oversights in the original statute. The 1980 act is significant not only because it was the product of cooperation between business and labor but also because it involved a coalition-building effort within the employer community. The deal struck gave some multiemployer plan sponsors gains at the expense of plan participants and other sponsors. However, since its enactment, the carefully knitted consensus has unraveled, threatening the future of the multiemployer pension system and potentially affecting the single employer system, too. Though the act has shored up the multiemployer insurance program, its passage has been a mixed blessing for business as a whole.

At the time that ERISA was passed, it seemed evident that single employer pension plans presented greater termination risks than multiemployer pension plans, since the bankruptcy of an independent company could jeopardize a plan's viability whereas in multiemployer plans there was strength in numbers—if one participating employer could no longer pay, the rest of the employers would pick up the unfunded liabilities.

This view overlooked the declining health of some industries in which multiemployer plans are dominant. In 1977, the Pension Benefit Guaranty Corporation reported that about 12 percent of multiemployer pension plans, covering about 20 percent of multiemployer plan participants (1½ million workers), were experiencing serious financial hardship that could lead to plan termination. The aggregate unfunded vested liabilities of these plans was estimated to exceed $3.8 billion.

The implementation of ERISA's insurance provisions for multiemployer plans (originally set for January 1978) seemed destined to aggravate the problem. Under the ERISA insurance program, ongoing plans would pay premiums to support beneficiaries of terminated plans. A high number of terminations would mean higher premiums, which would in turn encourage more terminations. The possibility that a domino effect could result in many plan terminations and the bankruptcy of the PBGC, leaving millions of retirees without pension protection, revived the business lobbyists' original criticism of the insurance proposal as unworkable.

Faced with this situation, Congress deferred the effective date of the multiemployer insurance provisions four times while weighing revisions of the legislation. Congress was saved from making difficult choices when organized labor and management came up with a compromise of their own. The unions agreed to a reduction in ERISA's protections of their members' benefits, and the employers agreed to much tougher employer liability provisions, faster funding schedules, and higher insurance premiums. The compromise won nearly unanimous support in Congress.

The prime mover behind the 1980 act was the AFL-CIO Building and Construction Trades Department. The department's president, Robert Georgine, also chairs the National Coordinating Committee for Multiemployer Plans, a coalition of unions involved in 140 multiemployer plans. Because of the already strong trend toward the open shop in the construction industry, the building trades unions were particularly concerned with the potential impact the multiemployer insurance program could have on the unionized sector of the industry. The National Construction Employers Council, representing employers who intended to remain in the union pension plans, likewise had a strong interest in shoring up the system. The unions were willing to accept exemptions from employer liability for the construction industry, and that proved to be the necessary sweetener. The NCEC in turn persuaded the national Chamber and the NAM to back the proposed bill. Though opinion was divided within each of the employer organizations, everyone stood to lose if the system broke down.

The multiemployer termination insurance issue involved conflicts between large and small employers. The former were concerned that, without stiff withdrawal liabilities, the smaller employers would withdraw from the plans and leave the large companies to foot the bills. Small employers argued that stiffer withdrawal liabilities would prevent the sale of small businesses and limit their ability to get credit.[19] The National Small Business Association won a number of key provisions, including the important de minimus rule, which provides that no liability will be assessed on a company if its withdrawal liability is less than a prescribed amount. A number of other groups, such as the entertainment, retail food, trucking, and bituminous coal industries, were also able to win special accommodations. Other multiemployer industries were not aware of the potential cost of the bill until it was too late.

The single employer plans wanted assurance that the multiemployer termination insurance system would be workable and self-sustaining so that it would not come looking for subsidies. In the process of coalition-building, an understanding was reached that if the single employer groups would support the multiemployer bill, then the multiemployer groups would lobby on behalf of single employer plans for reduced federal insurance coverage and against higher premiums.

The consensus in favor of the multiemployer plan termination insurance revision has dissipated since its enactment. The liabilities imposed on employers seeking to withdraw from multiemployer pension plans have proven to be serious burdens for many businesses. The law was intended to crack down on employers trying to avoid their obligations toward their employees' retirements; the critics argue that it is seriously affecting well-intentioned and responsible employers, too.

In 1981, a coalition of employers' organizations was formed to pursue further changes in the multiemployer insurance provisions of the law. It included the National Auto Dealers' Association, American Trucking Association, and the AGC and ABC as well as organizations representing food, apparel, and retail and wholesale grocery industries. Some of the coalition members had participated in the original 1980 agreement.

Consensus on remedies has been difficult to reach. One proposal would grant exemptions to individual industries, leaving the main statute substantially untouched. Some members of the coalition prefer an across-the-board approach that would remove virtually all multiemployer plans from ERISA's insurance provisions. However, other employer representatives are concerned that, without insurance, a large plan termination could lead to increased federal involvement in pensions and could stymie their efforts to remove or amend less radical proposals.

It is precisely the linkage between the multiemployer termination insurance issue and other ERISA reform issues (particularly in the single employer termination insurance program) that has thus far prevented the development of a new consensus on the former and substantial legislative progress on the latter. Large corporate employers, who tend to have single employer plans, view the controversy surrounding multiemployer insurance revision as a threat to passage of an omnibus pension reform bill, in which they have a much greater direct stake. A spokesman for the American Trucking Association commented: "We're sorry if the multi-employer bill endangers their chances. But our people are bleeding."[20]

ERISA Reform

The paperwork and cost burdens, the restrictions on established business practices, and the special problems created for small employers have long been at the top of the list of business complaints about ERISA. *Fortune* magazine has dubbed it "the most fiendish regulation of all."[21] Efforts to amend the law were introduced as soon as President Ford signed the bill, but consensus on specific proposals has been elusive even in the favorable climate of the Ninety-seventh Congress.

The basis for the call to deregulate the private pension system is the argument that ERISA has substantially increased the costs of providing pensions and, as a

Table 2
Defined Benefit Pension Plans
(in thousands)

	Formations	Terminations
1981	23.8	4.5
1980	18.8	4.3
1979	15.8	3.3
1978	9.7	4.6
1977	7.0	5.3
1976	4.8	9.0
1975	15.5	4.6

result, has discouraged employers from sponsoring plans. If private pension coverage is to expand, the argument goes, Congress must make pension plans more attractive and affordable for employers by reducing the burdens imposed by the law.

Developments immediately following the passage of ERISA bore out the employers' prediction that ERISA would discourage plan sponsorship. Defined benefit plans were the most seriously affected. Rough estimates of the number of new defined benefit plans have been made, based on the number of applications for qualified tax status filed with the Internal Revenue Service. The estimates show that plan formation dropped sharply when ERISA took effect, and only regained the 1975 level in 1979. Applications have increased steadily since then, reaching an all-time high of 24,000 in 1981. Plan terminations jumped sharply in 1976, exceeding the number of formations in that year; since that time, terminations have averaged about 4400 per year.[22] The short-term adverse impact of the law seems to have ended by 1978 (table 2).[23]

These statistics do not tell the whole story, however. Based on a 1977 survey of pension plans, the General Accounting Office concluded that economic and other factors played a more significant role than ERISA in decisions to terminate.[24] Samples of termination notices issued by the PBGC support the GAO contention. In 1978, for example, 25 percent of the terminating plans gave ERISA as the sole reason and 5 percent cited both ERISA and business reasons, whereas business conditions or considerations accounted for 70 percent of the terminating plans (which comprised 74 percent of the participants in plans that terminated that year).[25] ERISA has imposed costs on plan sponsors, but the GAO also found considerable benefits. The GAO concluded that as a result of the "act's passage many workers have a greater assurance of receiving benefits from their private pension plans."[26]

However, the costs due to ERISA have fallen disproportionately on small employers. A 1977 study of forty-eight Business Roundtable companies shows the impact of various regulations on costs. Though no small businesses were included in the sample, the findings have implications for them. The study found that, for the ten smallest employers, ERISA entailed average incremental costs per employee that were nearly seven times the costs for the ten largest employers.[27] The smaller employers have been burdened by ERISA relatively more than larger companies for two main reasons. First, because many of the legislated standards reflect practices of large corporate sponsors, more plan revision is necessary for small employers than large companies. Second, large companies have more resources to deal with the paperwork and plan provisions than do small and medium-sized companies.

Since ERISA's burdens have fallen disproportionately on small business, there has been considerable support in Congress for easing compliance with the requirements of ERISA, and even for completely exempting small employers from mandatory compliance. Many of the trade associations composed of larger firms have taken up the cause of the small employers in hope of reducing the burden on themselves in the process. For example, proposals for reduced reporting and disclosure requirements are aimed at helping small employers. The large employers support the changes, although producing summary annual reports and plan descriptions is not a major problem for them. It has also been proposed to exempt small plan sponsors from paying insurance premiums (though not from coverage); significantly, the large companies are less eager to go along with this idea.

Liberalization of the rules governing the management of pension funds by fiduciaries is a top priority of the banking and insurance industry associations and is also backed by plan sponsors. Small employers are primarily intent on raising the percentage of a fund's assets that can be invested in the sponsoring company, claiming that existing fiduciary standards have restricted their access to investment capital. Corporations and financial institutions have been pushing for a revision of the ''prohibited transaction'' section, which was designed to prevent fund trustees from doing business with parties having ties to the funds. The lobbyists have argued that the section has blocked many profitable and proper transactions and that the Department of Labor has been slow in granting exemptions.

The top priority of corporate employers is the overhaul of the single employer plan termination insurance program. The ERISA Industry Committee has been spearheading this drive, as its members have the biggest direct stake in the program's solvency—they pay approximately 85 percent of all the premiums collected. First, ERIC favors amending the provisions in the law that encourage companies to terminate adequately funded pension plans. This would involve increasing withdrawal liabilities significantly and changing the ''insurable event.'' Second, ERIC cites the precarious financial situation of the Pension Benefit Guaranty Corporation, primarily a result of poor economic conditions that have led a number of major corporations to the brink of plan termination. In April 1982, the PBGC recommended raising annual single employer premiums for covered employees from $2.60 to $6.00. Not surprisingly, ERIC and other employer groups have made clear they strongly prefer reducing the level and scope of benefit guarantees to raising premiums. Originally, PBGC guaranteed up to $700 monthly benefits. Indexing has doubled this amount since the law was passed. Small business lobbies have urged that only half of the indexing be added in the future.[28]

The employer's ERISA reform agenda has significant support in Congress. Although business seems to have regained the upper hand in setting the pension reform agenda, it remains unclear how successful it will be in overhauling the present law. Winning back what has been lost has proven difficult so far.

Seizing the Initiative

Business lobbies have come a long way since 1974. Not only have they recognized the value of working together, but the quality of their representation on pension issues has improved. It does appear unlikely that a bill as important as ERISA could appear again before the employer community without its representatives being thoroughly prepared for the event. The ERISA experience taught most employer organizations how costly legislation can be if they do not get involved in its drafting at the earliest stages.

ERIC concentrates on protecting the interests of large employers, but good public relations dictates that it also support the interests of small employers. The Chamber continues to maintain a higher visibility on retirement issues than the NAM, but all segments of the employer community have learned to coordinate more effectively with the segments of the pension industry that service their plans.

Though employers have compromised on some issues of federal pension policy regulation, they have generally been consistent. Business fought responsibility for insuring employees' pensions in 1974 and lost and reduction of this burden has remained a top priority on the employer organizations' pension agenda.

Business organizations prepared the groundwork for revising ERISA, but their efforts have been stymied during President Reagan's initial two years. Indeed, the only legislation enacted by the Ninety-seventh Congress affecting pensions included the liberalization of individual retirement accounts, which business lobbies favored, and a provision of the so-called Tax Equity and Fiscal Responsibility Act that reduced to $90,000 the annual pension maximum from a defined benefit plan. Of course, many business lobbyists opposed this provision.

The passage of an omnibus ERISA reform bill depends on a number of factors. First, should the recession result in the termination of pension plans of several major corporations, it could place the insurance program in jeopardy and prompt a major overhaul of ERISA.

Second, if the diverse business interests could reach a consensus on how to handle the multiemployer insurance program, their chances of revising other ERISA provisions—particularly the single employer insurance program—would be much improved. The inability of business lobbyists to reach a consensus on any specific set of provisions is probably the most important obstacle to the overhaul of ERISA.

Third, much depends on the kind of campaign mounted by the business community's opposition. It seems likely that reductions in benefit guarantees will elicit a major lobbying effort by the labor unions, senior citizen groups, and consumer groups. The AFL-CIO made it very clear that its support for the multiemployer bill "should not be construed as willingness to accept similar reductions in benefit guarantees for single employer plans."[29] Discussions concerning the overhaul of social security benefits have sensitized the public to retirement issues and suggest the difficulties business will face in persuading Congress to weaken private pension protections.

6

Unemployment Insurance: Persistence Pays Off

Nearly five decades ago, public policy in the United States firmly established the principle that employers have a financial responsibility for workers who are laid off through no fault of their own. The Social Security Act of 1935 required employers to insure their workers against the risk of temporary unemployment. Because of this responsibility, employer representatives have actively pursued legislative developments in unemployment insurance (UI).

With the exception of two states in which employees contribute to the UI funds, employers bear the bulk of the costs and consequently have a keen interest in keeping costs low. At the federal level, persistence, good organizations, unity, and relatively well thought out policy positions have all contributed to the employer lobby's success in influencing UI developments over nearly five decades.

The employer community's involvement with the federal UI program differs in a number of ways from its experience with private pension issues. First, employers recognized early the potential cost of an unemployment insurance program and organized to influence its development. Second, since business succeeded initially in shaping the structure of the UI program—particularly its federal-state structure—subsequent policy debates have been easier to fight. Third, because the Social Security Act created a new public program and did not try to regulate a preexisting system, there were fewer vested interests with which to deal. In the pension debate, the business community is divided between the banking, insurance, and pension industries and the plan sponsors. In the UI debate, business is relatively unified.

The Players

The Chamber of Commerce of the United States has been the most vocal of the employer organizations involved in federal UI legislation. The Chamber's policy committee on UI is the Council on Unemployment Compensation, consisting of representatives from major corporate members and from state chambers of commerce and technical experts. The UI group works closely with the Council of State Chambers of Commerce, a federation of thirty-four state business organizations that is primarily concerned with social security, UI, and workers' compensation payroll taxes. The typical employer represented by the Council of State Chambers of Commerce is a small-to-medium-size retailer, though its membership also includes manufacturers' organizations. Its activities are wholly funded by dues from member state organizations and corporate donations, the latter accounting for two-thirds of the total budget. The NAM also takes an active interest, though it has devoted only minimal staff time to the issue.

A number of trade associations have taken an interest in UI over the years, though the priorities of most associations change with agenda shifts on Capitol Hill. Retailers have long been concerned with UI; because theirs is a labor-intensive industry with a low-wage work force and high turnover, their UI costs tend to be high. The American Retail Federation, representing state and national retail associations, has also kept a watchful eye on UI developments for quite some time, though it is not the only retailers' association involved. Motivated by the recent high unemployment in their industry, the Associated General Contractors of America and the Associated Builders and Contractors have also joined the fray.

The national small business associations have not been extensively involved with unemployment insurance. The National Federation of Independent Business occasionally polls its members on UI issues and presents testimony. Unemployment insurance is not viewed as a small business issue, so it does not receive a significant share of the limited resources of small business organizations.

In line with its general approach, the Business Roundtable has maintained a low profile on UI matters. The UI policy interests of the largest corporate employers are already well looked after by UBA, Inc. (formerly Unemployment Benefit Advisors), which preceded the Roundtable by nearly three decades.

UBA differs from all the aforementioned organizations in that it is not, strictly speaking, a lobbying organization. Nonetheless, it is at the center of employer efforts to influence UI and workers' compensation policy. UBA acts in these two areas as a clearinghouse, conducts research and monitors developments, publishes bulletins, and briefs congressional staff members as well as employer representatives who are preparing to testify. UBA staff do not present testimony, though there is frequently a striking resemblance between the information contained in UBA bulletins and testimony presented by employer organizations.

J. Eldred Hill, Jr., has presided over UBA since June 1967. He is a member of both the Chamber and the NAM UI policy committees and serves as a consultant to other employer organizations, including the Business Roundtable, the National Industrial Council (a NAM affiliate), and the American Retail Federation. He is a former president of the Interstate Conference of Employment Security Agencies (an association of state employment security commissioners) and is widely recognized as a leading UI expert. As such, he is extremely influential in employer circles and elsewhere. On a promotional brochure distributed by UBA, the executive director of the National Industrial Council is quoted as saying: "I'm not 'gilding the lily' when I say that nobody from industry does anything on these subjects at a national level without checking with UBA first." This does not appear to be an overstatement.

UBA mainly represents large corporate employers. Its officers and directors include senior management figures from AT&T, Mobil Oil, U.S. Steel, and the like. UBA's membership overlaps considerably with those of the Chamber, the NAM, and the Business Roundtable because most large employers are members everywhere.

UBA traces its origins to 1933 when Wisconsin passed the first state UI law. Originally a profit-making organization, "the H & R Block of unemployment compensation," UBA advised companies on how to figure their UI payroll taxes and also represented the companies in the state capitol. Following the passage of the Social Security Act, UBA's clientele spread all over the country, and much of its lobbying was done in Washington. After the death of UBA's founder in 1945, the Wisconsin Manufacturers Association, with the help of other state employer organizations, established the company on a nonprofit basis to work exclusively as an employers' representative in Washington.

In June 1980, employers established an ad hoc working group composed of representatives from employers' associations. This group, which complements UBA's work and coordinates employer lobbying efforts, was formed to combat proposals made during the 1980 mini-recession to extend the duration of unemployment benefits beyond thirty-nine weeks. Although its origins were defensive, the working group subsequently advanced its own agenda and was very active in the events leading up to the passage of the UI provisions in the Omnibus Reconciliation Act of 1981. In 1982, the working group fought the further extension of UI benefits, but failed when the Reagan administration acquiesced to extending federal supplemental compensation by six to ten weeks to gain support for its proposed tax increases.

The System

The principal objective of the unemployment insurance program is to make up partially the lost earnings of temporarily unemployed workers who have lost their jobs through no fault of their own. The program is also designed to encourage stabilization of employment by making layoffs more expensive and to exert a countercyclical force in the economy by releasing purchasing power during economic recessions. Since there is so much at stake for both employers and workers, most national policy changes are hotly contested.

There have been as many as three tiers of UI programs. Most states provide eligible individuals unemployment benefits for up to twenty-six weeks. The extended benefits (EB) program, established in 1970, provides up to thirteen more weeks of benefits depending upon the level of unemployment in individual states. Temporary programs providing a third tier of benefits were enacted in 1971, 1974, and 1982. The emergency unemployment compensation program provided up to 13 more weeks of benefits to those who had exhausted regular and extended benefits from January through September of 1972. The federal supplemental benefits (FSB) program first provided up to thirteen weeks of benefits and then as much as twenty-six weeks during the period January 1975 through January 1978, and up to ten weeks in 1982–83.

The Social Security Act and the 1939 Federal Unemployment Tax Act (FUTA) provide the federal framework for the state UI programs. FUTA currently provides for a payroll tax of 3.5 percent on the first $7,000 in wages paid by an employer having at least one employee for twenty weeks in the year or having a quarterly payroll of at least $1,750. This effectively covers 97 percent of private wage and salary earners. If state programs meet federal requirements, employers are granted a 90 percent credit of the original 3 percent federal unemployment payroll tax. All states currently are in conformity with federal law.

States levy their own unemployment payroll taxes on employers on a taxable wage base at least as high as the one set by the federal government. These funds are used to pay benefits of the regular programs and the states' share of the extended benefits program. Unlike the federal tax, state rates are "experience-rated," that is, a company's taxes reflect its layoff experience.

Except for minimal federal standards, states have full autonomy in establishing substantive provisions for their UI programs. They set standards for benefit levels and duration, qualifying requirements, disqualifications, and penalties.

Table 3
Unemployment Compensation Benefits and Beneficiaries
(in billions)

Year	Regular	Extended benefits	Federal supplemental benefits	Total	Beneficiaries (millions)
1971	$ 5.0	$ .7	$—ᵃ	$ 5.6	6.6
1972	4.5	.5	.6	5.5	5.8
1973	4.0	.1	—	4.2	5.3
1974	6.0	.5	—	6.5	7.7
1975	11.8	2.5	2.1	16.4	11.2
1976	9.0	2.3	2.8	14.1	8.6
1977	8.3	1.8	1.3	11.4	8.0
1978	8.6	.7	—	9.4	7.6
1979	9.3	.3	—	9.5	\ 8.1
1980	14.5	1.7	—	16.2	10.0
1981	13.5	2.1	—	15.6	8.6
1982	19.3	1.9	—	21.2	11.4

Source: Unemployment Insurance Service, U.S. Department of Labor.
ᵃ less than 0.1

These provisions vary considerably from state to state, unlike minimum coverage and financing provisions, which are set at the federal level. Revenues from federal employment tax pay virtually all UI administrative expenses (both state and federal) and provide a loan fund from which states borrow when they lack funds for benefit payments. The balance between federal and state authority is a delicate one, and the impact of proposed national policy changes on the "federal-state partnership" is always keenly debated.

The extended benefits are financed equally through state and federal unemployment taxes. The benefits paid under the EB program are normally the same as those paid to recipients under their states' programs, but eligibility standards are determined by the federal government and EB duration is half the duration of regular benefits. Extended benefits must be paid to exhaustees of the regular program in a state when the regularly insured unemployment rate there is 5 percent and is also at least 20 percent higher than it was in the two preceding years. The supplemental benefits program, unlike the regular and extended benefits programs, is financed entirely by the federal government.

The regular state programs and the EB program do not cover federal employees. Civilian federal employees are covered by unemployment compensation for federal employees (UCFE), and veterans with recent service in the armed forces are covered by unemployment compensation for ex-servicemen (UCX). In addition, Congress has from time to time passed programs affecting specially designated groups. The most prominent of these programs was the trade readjustment assistance program, which provided benefits to workers unemployed as a result of increased imports resulting from liberalizations of American trade policy. The rationale for these special programs has been to compensate victims of federal policies.

The Principles: Controlling the Agenda

Business has adhered steadfastly to three guidelines for controlling the costs of UI: limit the scope of UI, minimize federal intervention with state regulation, and hold each company responsible for making up the funds that its unemployed workers have drawn from the system.

The employer community has insisted that the unemployment benefits program be limited to providing temporary income to laid-off workers seeking employment. The emphasis is on insurance rather than need. To minimize work disincentive effects, employers have advocated restrictive eligibility standards, modest benefit amounts, and limited duration. They have made it clear that a major policy goal is to differentiate between a temporary, unemployment *insurance* program and a need-based *welfare* program. Employers have argued successfully that they have assumed responsibility for financing the limited UI program only, leaving the responsibility for programs based on need to others.

A second major employer tenet in the UI policy debate is that unemployment insurance should be left to the states. This is an application of the subsidiarity principle, to wit, a higher unit of government should not undertake those tasks which can be performed as well or almost as well by a lower unit. Employers argue against federalization of the UI program on the grounds that the U.S. economy is too diversified to be centrally regulated, that states can best tailor the program to diverse local economic conditions, and that centralization will prevent the program from accomplishing its intended goals.

Third, the cornerstone of employer support for the UI program is the "pay-your-own-way" principle. Rejecting the concept that employers have the responsibility of being their brother's keepers, business representatives have insisted that employers pay the costs incurred by former employees only, and that they should not be expected to share UI costs for employees laid off by other companies. The primary means of implementing this principle is experience-rating, which bases each company's payroll tax liability on its costs to the system. Employers recognize that some portion of the costs is shared through the maximum and minimum tax rates, but they have fought to keep their "socialized" costs to a minimum.

These three principles have hardly gone unchallenged. Indeed, they have raised continuous debate. Billions of dollars are riding on the resolution of the controversies—the Department of Labor estimated outlays for UI in fiscal 1983 would reach a record of $30 billion. The application of the principles to the implementation of the system continues to raise complex political, social, and technical issues.

First, the concept of separating unemployment benefits from other income support programs assumes a carefully designed network dovetailing UI with other state and federal programs that meet the needs of the unemployed not covered by UI. This degree of coordination among social programs does not exist. The safety net that would conceptually justify the delineation between public responsibility and private responsibility is riddled with holes. In the United States there is no universal program to which workers can turn for assistance once they exhaust their unemployment benefits. In half the states, a family whose head is unemployed and living at home cannot qualify for welfare under Aid to Families With Dependent Children.

Second, the advantages of decentralizing control over social programs to states and localities may be offset by concomitant inequities. For example, two workers with identical employment and pay experience may be unevenly protected against the risk of unemployment just because they live or work in different states. Critics have suggested that other than philosophical arguments have led employers to champion the dominance of state control of UI regulations. It is difficult for any one state to raise its unemployment insurance taxes because this puts its employers at a competitive disadvantage vis-à-vis those in neighboring states who pay lower UI taxes. In the economic "war between the states" to attract jobs and investment, arguments that higher UI taxes might induce employers to relocate or prospective employers to locate elsewhere can be very persuasive not only with state legislators but even with unions concerned about the job security of their members. Even employers in states with liberal UI regulations believe there is little to be gained through federalization. Any federal standards would probably be based on the best (most costly) state practices, so federalization would merely relieve them of the influence they exert at the state level.

Third, the market-based approach to UI financing involves costs and benefits. Experience-rating has been rightly credited with encouraging employers to stabilize employment, but it has also strengthened the employers' resolve to contest claims for UI benefits filed by former employees. The social cost represented by disqualified claimants who do not find alternative means of support is frequently overlooked. Rather, their disqualification is lauded in the name of preventing abuse and maintaining the program's "integrity."

The Issues

Regardless of the social values underlying these three principles, they do constitute a reasonably consistent framework within which the UI program has evolved. Though the employers have lost the coverage debate, they have largely won the key battles concerning benefit adequacy, duration, eligibility, and financing. The policy issues in the UI debate have not changed fundamentally since the program's enactment.

Coverage

Employers have been least successful in holding the UI coverage line. Today the UI program covers 97 percent of the workforce, and there is continued effort to make the system universal by covering alien farm laborers, employees of smaller agricultural employers, and domestic workers in uncovered households. The debate centers, as it has in the past, on the trade-off between employees' need for coverage and issues of cost and feasibility. The main employer organizations, which now favor "maximum feasible coverage," only get involved with coverage issues if there is a possibility that newly covered employers cannot pay their own way.

Benefit Adequacy

A paramount issue in the UI debate has been whether to set a federal standard for the amount and duration of unemployment compensation. The business view has prevailed in every attempt aimed at strengthening and improving federal standards.

Fundamental to the controversy is the notion of adequacy. Traditionally, the accepted norm has been that UI should replace at least 50 percent of gross wages to avoid a drastic cut in the living standards of the laid-off worker. It has also been recognized that the lower the income bracket of the unemployed worker, the higher the replacement rate necessary to protect against severe economic hardship.

Consensus among policymakers has long been that benefits should be high enough so that a "great majority" (normally 80 percent) of a state's UI claimants have at least 50 percent of their income replaced. The National Commission on Unemployment Compensation found that in none of the states for which information was available did 80 percent of the beneficiaries receive half their weekly wage loss, and that in seven states fewer than 50 percent receive half their lost earnings. UI benefits were shown to be generally adequate for single workers who are not household heads, but least adequate for household heads who are the sole support of large families. The main reason for benefit inadequacy, according to the commission, is that maximum benefits have not risen with average wages.[1]

Employer representatives have taken issue with the commission's statistics, and prefer to measure the states' performance by other standards, such as failure to reduce maximum benefits in recessions, the number of increases in maximum benefits, and the number of states with automatic adjustments of the maximum to wage level changes.[2] Using those measures, they claim that states have lived up to their responsibilities in this area. They also insist that no single federal standard could achieve the 50/80 goal. They argue that a maximum of two-thirds of the state average weekly wage would be inadequate in some states and too high in others, so that state standards better meet the test of adequacy. Employers also warn against separating the UI taxing responsibility from benefit amounts. They argue that if the federal government determined the latter while states retained the power to set UI taxes, there would be little accountability and costs would skyrocket.

The standards controversy apart, employers generally caution against liberalizing benefits on the ground that reducing the cost of unemployment to the individual will be a disincentive to work. According to one estimate, a ten percent increase in replacement rates is accompanied overall by an increase of one-half to one full week in the duration of unemployment.[3] The work disincentive can be presumed to increase as individuals receive a larger proportion of their net pay in their unemployment checks. However, workers with higher replacement rates tend to be lower-paid individuals, who normally spend a higher percentage of their income on necessities and who would face considerable hardship if benefits were reduced.

Duration

Next to level of benefits, the duration of unemployment insurance has been one of the program's most controversial issues. Employers have favored benefits based on insurance principles, but have been forced to compromise over the years on the definition of temporary unemployment. Average potential duration of the regular program has increased from sixteen weeks in 1939 to twenty-four weeks in 1980, rising to as high as sixty-five weeks during the 1974–76 recession as a result of the combination of the extended benefits and federal supplemental benefits programs. In 1982, potential duration of benefits was extended to forty-nine weeks. Business has managed to ward off regular federal duration standards by arguing first that there is no need for them given the increase in average potential duration over the years, and second that no federal standard could adequately accommodate the various employment conditions among the states.

A key problem is the difficulty of defining temporary unemployment for the purposes of UI duration. Because the average duration of unemployment has been shown to vary directly with the unemployment rate, any determination of benefit duration is necessarily arbitrary. After the Second World War, high exhaustion rates in recessionary periods led to consideration of proposals to supplement the regular state UI programs. By the mid-1960s, the choice was between a program that would provide benefits based on the individual's unemployment history, regardless of general economic conditions, and a standby program that would be triggered during recessions. Organized labor pushed hard for a permanent program integrated with other labor market programs rather than one that triggered in and out with recessions.

Business won the debate. It argued that relatively few claimants are likely to draw benefits beyond twenty-six weeks under favorable economic conditions. Providing extended benefits at all times, business claimed, would be both costly and subject to abuse. By instituting a standby program, temporary benefit extension became a function of economic conditions. Both the extended benefits and federal supplemental benefits programs were instituted on this basis. The continuing controversy over the level and calculation of the trigger is indicative of the lack of consensus as to when increased duration is warranted.

Today, employers accept full responsibility for financing extended benefits, though this has not always been the case. The difficulty lies in attempting to apportion responsibility for a claimant's unemployment between the employer who ordered the layoff and the unfavorable economic conditions that may prolong the period of forced idleness. The Council of State Chambers of Commerce summarized the employers' position:

> It has been a historic position of the employer community that benefits provided to the unemployed beyond 26 weeks should not be financed by employer payroll taxes. Nevertheless in recent years the employer community generally supported the enactment of temporary 13-week benefit programs financed from payroll taxes. It has been the position that when the unemployment extends beyond 39 weeks, the financing of benefits should be considered to be a general obligation of society and attributable more to poor economic conditions and lack of job opportunities rather than to the initial termination of employment.[4]

Business organizations are opposed to the extension of unemployment benefits beyond thirty-nine weeks, though the vigor of their protest depends on economic conditions. During the depth of the mid-1970s recession and in 1982, employers tended not to contest the need for an extension but opposed the idea of having business foot the bill. Employers are generally agreed that if politics dictate duration beyond thirty-nine weeks, the third tier should be wholly financed as a welfare measure by general revenues separate from the federal-state system. That is, employers favor federal financing of the supplementary benefits but are prepared to assume responsibility for extended benefits. The 1982 extension of federal supplemental benefits was financed entirely from general revenues.

Eligibility

The general employer approach to eligibility issues has been to oppose federal intervention and to favor tighter state eligibility standards and stiffer penalties. Most employers defend tight eligibility criteria as a means of saving money and maintaining the integrity of the UI program without cutting benefit levels or duration for those who are truly deserving. Employers in construction, needle trades, and other seasonal industries usually depart from the party line on eligibility. Most employers in seasonal industries prefer looser work tests and use unemployment compensation as a supplement to the wage structures in their industries.

Controversy over eligibility issues centers on the application of generally accepted criteria. The major criteria include a strong attachment to the labor force for a specified number of weeks and/or amount of earnings and availability for suitable work. Other important eligibility issues concern the conditions of the claimant's separation from work; for example, eligibility can be denied if the claimant quit work voluntarily or was fired for just cause. To qualify for extended benefits in some states, claimants are expected to have worked a greater number of weeks than they need to have worked to qualify for regular benefits. This is justified on the ground of maintaining a consistent relationship between the duration of work and benefits.

The determination of suitable work engenders further controversy. Some have argued that the concept should be broadened for extended benefits claimants by requiring them to accept work that would be considered unsuitable for claimants of regular benefits with the same levels of skills and experience. The justification for the application of harsher standards for the long-term unemployed is that they may not find jobs paying the rates they received prior to the layoff. This view has been attacked both as unduly harsh on individual claimants who happen to become unemployed during recessionary periods and as wasteful of their skills. The employers' viewpoint on eligibility for extended and supplementary benefits has gained currency in recent years. Federal eligibility requirements for the EB and FSB programs have been tightened since 1977.

Financing

The "bottom line"—program cost and financing—is by far the most important UI issue to the employers. Though organized labor has strongly objected to experience-rating, questioning its effectiveness in stabilizing employment and also questioning the desirability of encouraging employer stakes in UI administration, business has won this battle. Federal law requires experience-rating in order for a state to qualify for the tax credit, though state provisions vary widely. Most employer organizations favor rigorous application of experience-rating. They have not only opposed the recent rising costs of "socialized" state programs—costs not charged to the unemployment fund and not to individual employers—but have also favored experience-rating the federal unemployment tax.

The two primary influences on employers' UI taxes are the tax rate and the taxable wage base. There has been a continuous debate since the passage of the first state UI law about whether to raise the rate or base when additional revenues are needed. This has traditionally been the most divisive issue within the employer community. The interest of low-wage employers in raising the tax base rather than the rate is obvious. Employers who pay higher rates have argued that adjusting the rate and leaving the base unchanged distributes the burden of higher UI costs more equitably because all employers have to pay the same increase. Congress has tended to resolve this conflict among employer groups by raising the taxable wage base and rate simultaneously.

The liberal-labor lobbies have called for a rise in the wage base, as Congress has done in the case of social security, arguing that the decrease of taxable wages as a percentage of total wages has resulted in a relative contraction of resources available for financing UI. From 1940 to 1977, this ratio declined from 98 percent to 45 percent. The national commission in 1980 urged setting the base at 65 percent of wages. The commission held that it was unfair for low-wage employers to be taxed on a greater proportion of the wages they paid than were high-wage employers, and that raising the tax rate would only worsen these inequities.[5] The unions have long argued for parity with the social security wage base on the ground that previous earnings determine the level of payments. As of 1983, the UI taxable wage base was $7,000, compared with $35,700 for social security. There are persuasive reasons for having different taxable bases for the two programs, but they do not necessarily justify the wide differential in coverage.

State self-sufficiency in UI financing underlies employer opposition to most plans for reinsurance of state UI programs and all schemes for cost-equalization, which would involve federal subsidies to states experiencing unusually high UI costs as measured by a norm applicable to all states.[6] Cost-equalization would also result in increased costs for low-cost states and relief for high-cost states. Employers fear that it would reduce states' accountability for their own costs and would weaken the incentive for states to keep a tight rein on costs. Business has argued that there is no need for cost-equalization because the federal-state system of financing is basically sound, and it maintains that liberal benefit and eligibility rules are as much to blame for the difficulties of high-cost states as are high unemployment rates. Supporters of cost-equalization have argued, thus far unsuccessfully, that such a plan is needed to relieve the pressure on states to underfinance their UI programs as a result of interstate competition for jobs and investment.

The business community, then, has been notably successful in its attempt to keep the UI policy debate within parameters that it finds manageable. For the most part, its views about the role of the UI program have prevailed. With the exception of the wage base versus rate controversy, the employer lobbies have been remarkably united on most UI issues and have been supported by very effective and sustained lobbying at the federal level.

The 1965–66 Round: Employers Unite to Defeat Labor's Bill

The proposed 1965 Johnson administration amendments (HR8282), which called for a much increased federal role in state programs and for a new extended benefits program, framed the policy debate on UI for years to follow. The ensuing developments demonstrated the ability of the business lobbies both to win a crucial legislative battle against all political odds and to shift the debate largely onto their own turf. In the course of the debate, employer organizations proposed a conservative alternative (HR1519) to the administration bill, which represented the first employer lobby consensus in favor of a UI reform bill. The lobby's ability to present a positive alternative to the proposals backed by the Johnson administration and organized labor was instrumental in defeating those proposals in the most liberal Congress in recent decades. The 1965–66 battle was an important take-off point for employers in the UI arena.

The most controversial proposals in HR8282 were the federal standards for the regular programs. The bill provided that all eligible claimants would be entitled to weekly benefits equal to 50 percent of their average weekly wage up to a maximum of 50 percent of the state average weekly wage; that all eligible claimants would be entitled to at least twenty-six weeks of benefits; that employees would not be required to work more than twenty weeks in order to qualify for regular benefits; that extended benefits of up to twenty-six weeks (for a total duration of fifty-two weeks) would be available, regardless of economic conditions; and that the federal standard requiring the use of experience-rating by the states would be abolished. The bill also would have extended coverage to an additional five million workers. To pay for these program extensions, HR8282 provided not only for increased payroll taxes but also for a federal contribution to finance a wage-equalization program.

Employer organizations reacted to the proposals early and with vigor. The focus of the employer campaign against the Johnson bill was the House Ways and Means Committee, chaired by Wilbur Mills, who was sympathetic to the employers' view. In April 1965, even before HR8282 was introduced, Stanley Rector, then head of UBA, started the ball rolling in UBA's newsletter, The *Advisor*:

> We have been waiting, in a sense, 'to see the whites of their eyes' before getting off our first volley. . . . The risks of waiting further for an exact knowledge of the measure's content are at this stage con-

siderably outweighed by the risks of a fully-greased operation which
has characterized the eminently successful legislative performance of
the President: both as majority leader and in his present incumbency.[7]

UBA then proceeded to set out employer rebuttals to virtually every administration proposal. UBA urged business groups to coordinate their testimony so
as to demonstrate the potential impact of HR8282 on a state-by-state basis.
About seventy employer organizations and individual corporations testified
and about a hundred more, representing a wide cross-section of areas and
industries, submitted statements for the record.

The Interstate Conference of Employment Security Agencies (ICESA)
supported the employer position on HR8282. Ties between employers and state
UI administrators have traditionally been close at the national level because of
the ever-present threat of federalization. ICESA representatives also gained
access to the executive deliberations, so the employers' viewpoint received an
extensive airing *in camera*. The outcome of these deliberations was HR15119.
The employer lobby got virtually all of the "offensive" features of HR8282
removed. The *Congressional Quarterly* characterized the efforts as the most
effective employer lobbying campaign since the enactment of the Taft-Hartley
Act in 1947.[8]

Notable among the employer victories was the absence of all federal standards concerning benefit amounts, duration, and qualifying employment in the
reported bill. The permanent twenty-six-week extended benefits program had
been eliminated and replaced with a triggered, recession-based program providing thirteen weeks of added benefits. The cost-equalization proposal had
been dropped, the effective federal requirement that states experience-rate their
UI taxes was preserved, the coverage provision for employees of small employers was made less all-embracing, and the provision covering hired farm
labor was dropped altogether. HR15119 passed the House by a vote of 374 to
10.

The employers' strategy in the Senate was to protect the gains they had made
in the House. HR15119 was not perfect by employers' standards. They preferred more restricted extended benefits, lower tax rate and wage base increases, and the elimination of federal disqualification standards, which they
thought set a bad precedent. Nonetheless, all the major employer organizations
came out in support of the bill's passage without amendment. This eminently
pragmatic stance stemmed from the employers' concern that if the carefully
balanced compromise bill were upset, the opposition might succeed in passing
less palatable legislation.

Legislators recognized that this was the first time employers had united to
push through a bill of their own. In a revealing exchange between Mr. Paul
Henkel and Mr. William Brown of the Council of State Chambers of Com-

merce and members of the Senate Finance Committee, the employers' unusual solidarity was noted:

Mr. Henkel: Surely it is no secret that employers throughout the country were forced by the extreme provisions of HR8282 to rise up in protest. It should be significant, therefore, that business and industry is coming forward at this time to support HR15119 despite the fact that some of its important provisions are not consistent with the views of the employer community.

Senator Gore: May I ask a question here?

Senator Talmadge: Yes.

Senator Gore: Isn't this the first time that the business community has given its support to an unemployment compensation bill?

Mr. Henkel: As a whole bill, sir, perhaps that is true. I would imagine that there have been previous times where business and industry have supported portions of a bill.

. . . .

Mr. Brown: If I might add, Mr. Chairman, I believe there was some legislation some years ago regarding the Reed loan fund which had general business support, but they have not generally supported federal changes. It is quite common for business groups to support improvement in State laws at the State level.[9]

Employer unity was not, however, quite enough to protect the bill from amendments in the Senate. The Johnson administration and organized labor scored an important victory when they got the Senate Finance Committee to reinstate federal standards governing benefit amount, duration, and qualifying employment. The Senate version also provided for a higher FUTA tax rate and higher wage base than did the House bill, provided complete federal funding for the extended benefits program, and extended coverage to some farm labor.

The three-day Senate debate focused almost exclusively on the issue of federal standards, which the Senate approved with some revisions by a vote of 53 to 31. Efforts of Senate supporters to get the bill to conference were ignored by the bill's opponents in the House for more than two months. The conferees finally met twice shortly before adjournment. Employers applied considerable pressure on the conferees to reject the standards included in the Senate version, to which labor's supporters held fast. The resulting impasse was a disappointment to organized labor, which had lobbied the White House heavily on the issue.

The *Advisor* of October 21, 1966 was headlined: "RIP: The Unemployment Insurance Amendments of 1965; Born: May 19, 1965; Died: October 21, 1966." The *Advisor* commented, "We consider the outcome of *no bill at all* to be a complete victory."[10] However, the bill's defeat meant that the need for an overhaul of the system remained and employers would have to fight the same battle again in a few years. Employers would have an advantage in the next round, though, because it would take place under a friendlier administration.

The 1969–70 Round: Employers Score Again

The 1969–70 round was an even greater victory for the employer community. The Nixon administration proposals (HR12625) largely reflected the employers' priorities. The proposed extended benefits program was to be activated by a national trigger based on the insured unemployment rate and to provide up to thirteen weeks of benefits in the same amount as the regular state programs. It was to have been financed completely by raising the FUTA tax rate. The Nixon administration also proposed reforms of the regular state programs. Notable among these were the proposals to extend coverage and to include federal standards governing eligibility for regular benefits.

It is significant that in 1969 the Nixon administration did not propose federal benefit standards. It appears that the Department of Labor urged such standards but employer lobbies were successful in deleting the proposal. Instead, President Nixon appealed to the states to raise benefit levels voluntarily to eliminate the need for a federal benefit standard.[11]

Although the employer organizations supported the objectives of the administration bill, they still sought to change it even more to their liking. First, employers persuaded the Ways and Means Committee to retain the federal taxable wage base at $4,200. Second, they fought off amendments calling for federal benefit standards, and succeeded in adding a long sought provision for judicial review. Third, they succeeded in substituting equally shared federal/state financing of the extended benefits program for 100 percent federal financing. Fourth, they got the farm coverage provision eliminated. The House approved the committee bill (HR14705) by a vote of 337 to 8.

The business lobbies were also reasonably successful in the Senate Finance Committee. The committee defeated a motion to impose federal benefit standards and an effort to finance the extended benefits program completely with FUTA revenues. It also rejected the small employer coverage provisions, which the employers opposed. The farm coverage provision, however, was adopted.

UBA rallied its troops with the call "Next the Senate Floor—Or, On Moving the Piano One More Time." The most important fight on the Senate floor was against amendments for federal benefit standards. The *Advisor* said, "If we are successful, the last major hurdle will have been crossed. *If we fail, then we must mount an immediate and intensive fight to kill the bill.*"[12] The Senate obliged. Crowed UBA on August 13, 1970: "It took 5 years, 2 months, and 22 days, but we now have reasonable amendments to the Federal-State unemployment compensation law on the statute books. . . . Monday, August 10, 1970—the day President Nixon signed HR 14705 into law—signalled the accomplishment of virtually everything we had sought through these five long years."[13] Victors are wont to exaggerate, and membership organizations need to show results to keep their clientele. However, this appraisal was not far from the truth.

Lost Ground: 1971–74

The business lobbies' string of victories ran out in the early 1970s, primarily because the rise in and lengthening duration of unemployment put pressure on Congress to extend the two-tiered UI system. First came the 1971 Emergency Unemployment Compensation Act, which provided a temporary third tier of unemployment benefits to claimants in states with unemployment above the extended benefits trigger level. After the 1971 emergency program expired, Congress enacted the federal supplemental benefits program.

The employers were between a rock and a hard place when it came to dealing with calls for a third tier, particularly in December 1974, when unemployment was hitting levels unseen since the 1930s. Public opinion was very much in favor of doing something for the unemployed, and the business lobbies were hard put to argue against the extensions. Instead, they argued that if an extension was necessary, it should be financed out of general revenues rather than charged to employers. On a practical level, they pointed out that the federal extended unemployment compensation account was already heavily in debt. On principle, they objected to funding more than thirty-nine weeks on the grounds that such benefits were no longer unemployment insurance, but welfare.

Employers lost the first couple of rounds in December 1974 and March 1975: first the federal supplemental benefits program was enacted, and then thirteen more weeks of potential duration were added. But they recouped their losses in June 1975, when the federal trigger for the FSB program was eliminated, and in April 1977, when potential duration was cut back to thirteen weeks, eligibility tightened, and general revenue financing provided for the remaining months of the program. The 1977 battles were primarily exercises in damage control from the employers' point of view; complete victory would have entailed blocking the program's extensions.

Business was rather less concerned about the supplemental unemployment assistance (SUA) program enacted in December 1974. This initially provided up to twenty-six weeks of unemployment benefits (later extended to thirty-nine weeks) to about eight million state and local government employees and two million domestic and agricultural workers not previously covered by the federal-state system. While the employers' organizations opposed these provisions in principle, they acquiesced because the SUA program was financed with general revenues and did not involve a direct tax burden on them.

The 1975–76 Round: Cutting the Losses

Some of the debate over FSB extensions was caught up in a broader UI reform discussion that predated the energy crisis recession. However, the drain of the 1974–76 recession on the trust funds added important financing issues to the reform agenda and a certain urgency to the debate. The main issues of the 1975–76 round were financing, the EB triggers, and the perennial question of federal benefit standards, though extended coverage and eligibility restrictions were important issues, too.

The administration proposed covering an additional six million workers in the UI system, raising the federal taxable wage base as well as the FUTA tax rate, and adding a federal benefit standard. The bill (HR8614) also liberalized the state trigger for the extended benefits program and recalculated the national extended benefits trigger.

Congressman James Corman of California, chairman of the newly established Subcommittee for Public Assistance and Unemployment, introduced a more liberal proposal (HR8366). First, it covered about the same number of domestics and state and local government employees, but a much greater number of farm workers. Second, it set the maximum benefit for the regular program at three-fourths of the state average weekly wage. Third, it eliminated the triggered extended benefits program altogether, requiring that a total potential duration of fifty-two weeks of benefits be available to claimants in all states, and limited the amount of work that could be required for qualifying for any benefits. Finally, it proposed to raise the federal UI taxable wage base to the level of the social security taxable wage base.

Employer representatives devoted much of their testimony before the House Ways and Means subcommittee to arguments against the proposed federal benefit standards. One employer representative from the Council of State

Chambers of Commerce suggested that the unions were supporting a higher federal benefit standard than the administration proposed precisely to make the latter proposition appear "moderate and reasonable, and a likely compromise. Employers do not buy this ploy," he said.[14] UBA commented in a similar vein.

Employers were preoccupied with three objectives when the bill came before the Ways and Means Committee: (1) fending off the impending drive for federal benefit standards; (2) getting the proposed federal taxable wage base of $8,000 reduced; and (3) preventing the liberalization of the state trigger for extended benefits. They were only moderately successful in the pursuit of these goals. They were initially unable to get a reduction in the proposed federal taxable wage base or in the state extended benefits trigger, but they defeated the reinsertion of federal benefit standards by a vote of 18 to 17.

The Ways and Means Committee reported out HR 10210 to the House under a closed rule in May 1976. It was voted down and sent back to the committee. Organized labor opposed it because it included no federal benefit standards, the employers disliked it because of the $8,000 taxable wage base and the liberalized EB trigger, and state and local government officials did not want to pay for the coverage of their employees. However, the bill was brought to the floor again a month later, this time under a modified closed rule. Employers managed again to beat a federal benefit standard amendment and succeeded in passing an amendment reducing the federal taxable wage base from $8,000 to $6,000. Coverage of state and local employees was passed, as were a couple of restrictive eligibility standards. Employers as a group, though generally opposed to these last two amendments, were only indirectly interested in them. The House passed the bill 237–157.

The business community was, overall, quite pleased with the House bill. Michael Romig of the national Chamber of Commerce commented that "perhaps the most significant factor" in the House passage of the bill "was that . . . the business community has been bombarding Capitol Hill with communications. . . . The Democrats went off to their convention and came back to a stack of mail."[15]

Employers wanted to trim the bill even more in the Senate. They sought to reduce the $6,000 federal taxable wage base even further and to drop the provisions for a new EB trigger. Some segments of the employer community wanted to eliminate the provisions for expanded coverage. Business was also opposed to the creation of a national commission on unemployment compensation. Though the idea had originally been attractive to employers as a means of forestalling federal legislation, once it was coupled with impending legislation there was concern that it would eventually lead to the enactment of numerous federal standards for the regular state programs.

The Senate Finance Committee did not disappoint the business lobbyists, though it did not give them all they wanted. The conference version blunted most of the restrictions added by the Senate Finance Committee. The employer community was reasonably successful in reworking the original reform proposals to its satisfaction. As it turned out, 1976 was the last chance for the liberal-labor coalition to achieve federal benefit standards for a long time to come.

The Cost-saving Crusade

Employers and their congressional allies had some success in bringing attention to UI cost issues in the late 1970s. Moreover, their gains during the Carter administration were only preliminary to much sharper cuts carried out during President Reagan's first year in office. In 1978, advocates of cutting UI costs—which was discreetly couched in terms of "saving costs" rather than "eliminating benefits"—won a new ally with the election of Governor David Boren of Oklahoma to the Senate and his subsequent appointment to chair the Senate Finance Subcommittee on Unemployment and Related Problems. Senator Boren became the employers' major supporter on UI questions, a role abandoned by Representative Wilbur Mills in 1974.

In March 1980, Senator Boren won Senate approval for some of his cost-savers. His amendments eliminated the national trigger for the extended benefits (EB) program, permitted the use of stricter state EB triggers, and tightened eligibility for the military (UCX) and EB programs. The House conferees rejected the Boren amendments and the bill died in conference. UBA's epitaph for the bill was "Too Good To Be True."[16] Another attempt to rein in UI costs was passed by the Senate in October 1980. The House refused to accept the Senate amendments, and the bill was scheduled for conference after the election. The conference committee never met during the lame duck session.

Senator Boren and his business backers succeeded, however, in including UI cost-savers in the Omnibus Reconciliation Act of 1980. The most important of these cost-saving provisions disqualified persons who refuse suitable employment from receiving EB, tightened the definition of suitable work, and denied EB to persons who leave work voluntarily or are fired for misconduct. The projected decrease in federal UI costs was in excess of $200 million in fiscal 1981. The conferees could not agree to Senate proposals either to eliminate the national EB trigger or to allow states to set a more restrictive mandatory EB trigger. These major changes would have to wait another year until Congress adopted the Reagan administration's economic recovery program, which represented a major shift in federal policy on UI.

In August 1981, Congress approved major cuts in the domestic budget at President Reagan's urging. The 1981 Reconciliation Act contained several changes in UI. The cuts eliminated the national EB trigger (reinstated a year later); raised the mandatory and optional state triggers for the EB program; excluded EB recipients from the count of the insured unemployment rate; required 20 weeks' work to qualify for extended benefits; and further tightened eligibility for military programs (later rescinded). One administration proposal that was not passed was a federal standard that would have required claimants who had collected thirteen weeks of benefits to accept jobs paying at least their weekly benefit amount or the minimum wage. This was similar to the 1980 "suitable work" requirement Congress imposed on claimants of extended benefits. Although the emphasis of the Reagan budgetary proposals was on the reduction of federal intervention, the administration was willing to violate its principles in this case.

The debate concerning the proposed cuts in the UI program centered more on concerns for budget-balancing and cost-saving than it did on consideration of the impact of these cuts on the labor market. To some degree, this was the result of the relatively new reconciliation procedure, which made substantive changes in program content part of the budget process.

The employer community generally backed the administration's UI proposals; indeed, most of those ideas had made their first appearance in employer representatives' testimony in previous years. However, most employers balked at the idea of a federal suitable work requirement being imposed on the regular state programs. The Chamber, despite its steadfast support for the Reagan economic program, did voice a mild reservation: "The U.S. Chamber supports the philosophy behind the Administration proposal. We prefer that it be implemented through voluntary state action rather than federal legislation."[17] As recently as 1979, the Chamber had opposed such a requirement on the grounds that it encroached unjustifiably on the states' jurisdiction. The NAM was also uncomfortable with this proposal: "NAM philosophically opposes any legislative provisions which impose federal eligibility standards on individual state unemployment compensation programs."[18] The UBA also singled out the suitable work proposal as the only element of the president's UI program that it did not support, calling it "a wholly unnecessary and unwise federal benefit standard."[19]

Employers' singular lack of enthusiasm for the federal suitable work standard for the regular program eventually led to its being dropped. Otherwise, Congress adopted the administration proposals with only slight modification. The Senate Finance Committee also included some new provisions tightening the federal loan policy toward state UI trust funds. The House managed to liberalize the Senate's loan reform provisions to the benefit of a number of states that were heavily in debt to the federal government. UBA indicated reservations about the new loan policy but on balance was well satisfied with the results. "Qualification for stretched out repayment is too easy, and provisions to encourage solvency and discourage borrowing are weak; but it was a bargain price for the total package.''[20] The cuts in the EB, UCX, and trade adjustment assistance programs saved an estimated $3 billion in fiscal 1982 alone. These cuts were the largest ever made in these programs.

The Omnibus Reconciliation Act of 1981 represented the most sweeping implementation of employer priorities in the history of the UI program. Though it did not exhaust the employers' wish list of UI-related cuts, it did meet the employers' demands to a greater extent than had been previously thought politically feasible. However, it cannot be concluded that the Reagan administration and business community had identical priorities. The administration's support for the federal suitable work requirement is a case in point; the Reagan team proposed to go further than even the business community thought desirable. A second example is the 12-percent cut in federal grants to states for UI administrative costs, which was also included in the act. Employers had quietly expressed misgivings about these cuts. Both employers and states viewed the administration's call for greater efficiency on the part of state employment agencies as unrealistic. These funds were restored in 1982.

Even before employers could fully savor the fruits of their 1981 victory, the economic tide turned against them. Less than one year after the passage of the 1981 Reconciliation Act, the Reagan administration was forced to retreat on its supply side ideology and to petition Congress for tax increases that included boosts in the unemployment insurance tax base (from $6,000 to $7,000) and federal tax rate (from 0.7 percent to 0.8 percent). The extra taxes were to finance supplemental unemployment benefits ranging from six to ten weeks. These were later extended by another two to six weeks, depending upon the state insured unemployment rates. To be sure, the Reagan administration continued to oppose supplementary unemployment benefits, arguing in the face of the highest unemployment since the Great Depression that the idea is ''inequitable, ill-timed, and costly.'' Nonetheless, the Reagan administration supported the extension of the benefits and the higher taxes as part of its 1982 tax boost.

The Outlook: 1983 and Beyond

A key question is how business and its political allies will use their current advantage. Some employer tacticians may be tempted to take advantage of the conservatives' new-found strength at the national level and press ahead with new federally legislated UI program restrictions. The Chamber, for one, had a revised agenda out within twelve days of the signing of the 1981 Reconciliation Act, asking for more.[21] It is possible, too, that the employer community might turn to federal standards as a means of cutting back on the regular programs.

That would stand on its head the traditional relationship of liberal federalizers and conservative states' rights advocates. It is unlikely, though, because employer organizations cannot ignore long-run effects, and what the Reagan-dominated Ninety-seventh Congress gave, another Congress may take away. A more realistic policy for employer lobbyists is to keep the federal role in UI to a minimum and to concentrate on securing cutbacks in the states. In December 1980, the business organizations concerned with UI issues organized the first national gathering of employer representatives dedicated to coordinating an approach to UI issues in the states.

In the short run, business organizations have to deal with a recession that has exacerbated the deficit of the federal-state UI system. There is an urgent need for a much-increased federal taxable wage base, and a persuasive case can be made for a reinsurance plan to protect high-unemployment states against long and deep recessions. By early 1983, nearly half the states owed the federal treasury a total of $11 billion that they had borrowed to pay unemployment benefits, and their deficits were rising. Simple tinkering with the federal loan policy will not restore the system's fiscal soundness.

Beyond the recession, demands for correction of the 1980–81 excesses are likely to persist. For example, the redefinition of suitable work, if enforced, may have placed considerable hardship on individual claimants and resulted in a senseless waste of resources for society as a whole. It is better economics to subsidize longer job searches for skilled workers than to require them to take minimum wage jobs. More generally, requiring EB claimants to meet higher eligibility tests than claimants of regular benefits is unreasonable in light of the longer duration of unemployment during a recession. Surely there is some room for policy based on claimants' needs next to the hallowed principles of insurance.

More resources should also be devoted to tightened administration of the UI program. In 1979, detected overpayments amounted to $128 million (including $47 million in fraudulent overpayment) and were rising. According to a study prepared for the National Commission on Unemployment Compensation, the losses were incurred in part because state unemployment offices lack the resources to administer the program properly.[22] Employers are right to complain about UI fraud and abuse, but improving program administration—not tightening eligibility—is the way to protect the program's integrity.

Persistence, good organization, and a relatively unified approach have paid off for employers in the federal UI policy area. By pursuing its legislative goals doggedly and with a basically sound strategy, the business community has been able to keep the UI program remarkably close to its intended goal. Business has been able to blunt most drives for expanding the scope of the UI system by offering alternative ways—albeit usually the least costly—to change the program. By influencing the way change has been brought about, employers have been able to keep the policy debate largely on their own terms. The best example of this was their victory in 1970, when the choice was made between a permanent and a triggered EB program. In subsequent years, they have even been able to craft the EB triggers to their specifications.

The employer lobbies have also won most of the other major policy issues in the past fifteen years. They have blocked federal standards for benefit amounts and have kept the UI federal taxable wage base far below the level of the social security taxable wage base. They have also fended off proposals for cost-equalization and reinsurance and have managed to keep the federal unemployment insurance tax rate at a relatively modest level. The only issue on which employers have lost is coverage, which now includes 97 percent of the private work force.

The business lobbies' UI win-loss record has, on the whole, been quite good. In 1965–66, during the tenure of the most liberal administration and Congress in recent decades, it defeated a major effort to expand the system. In 1969–70, the employer community again succeeded in shaping a reform bill to its satisfaction. The early 1970s represented significant employer losses, with potential UI duration temporarily extended to sixty-five weeks. The 1976 amendments expanded the program considerably but could also be considered an employer victory; employers were able to cut their losses by beating back federal benefit standards, a higher taxable wage base, a more liberal EB trigger, and by watering down an extensive coverage provision. The dawn of the 1980s, of course, brought major triumphs for the employer UI lobby.

Contrary to popular expectation, the expansions of the UI system have occurred during the Nixon and Ford years rather than during Democratic administrations. Major reform was defeated under Johnson in 1966; a third tier of UI, defeated under Carter in 1980, was added temporarily two years later when Reagan reluctantly approved it.

Employers and their organizations have proven to be quite proficient at capitalizing on public sentiment favorable to their cause, but generally unable to shift public opinion when it is in the other camp. Public opinion on UI matters, not surprisingly, responds rather directly to the national unemployment rate. The victory in 1965–66 was certainly helped by the relatively low national unemployment rate at the time. Similarly, in 1982 employers could not stem the clamor for further extension of UI benefits, and the Reagan administration (prodded by Congress) could not ignore the tremendous public concern about the high levels of unemployment and the needs of millions who had exhausted their regular and extended benefits. The victories won by the Reagan White House in 1981 were relinquished, however, two years later even before the accession of an administration more sympathetic to the needs of the unemployed.

7

Labor Law and Union Power: Employers Win Big

Nothing unites the employer community like a good squabble with organized labor over issues relating to union power. The history of the business community's political involvements is replete with divisions over numerous economic issues, but when the "social" or "labor" question moves from the economic sphere to labor-management relations, employers close ranks. Heated arguments are standard fare when amendments to the National Labor Relations Act are considered by Congress.

Legislative battles involving union power issues are almost invariably won by the business community, unlike other kinds of labor issues such as programs designed to benefit individual workers. With the exception of the Wagner Act, employers have had the upper hand in every attempt to reform federal labor laws. Questions surrounding the collective rights of workers vis-à-vis management elicit emotional reactions within the employer and labor camps, inducing each side to overcome internal differences and rally to the cause. The mobilization of employers' resources in such cases has paid off; repeatedly, business lobbyists have successfully exploited the persistent emotionalism over the labor issue to the disadvantage of the unions. Business has managed to capture the political center on questions of union power through well-orchestrated public information campaigns, whereas labor representatives have tended to isolate themselves by rigidly defending their rights.

Two major battles involving union power issues have occurred since the passage of the 1959 Landrum-Griffin Act. These encounters concerned common situs picketing legislation in 1975 and labor law reform two years later.

Brian Linder prepared a partial earlier draft of this chapter.

The latter was by far the more important event and displayed the power of a unified and well-oiled business lobby. The employers' victory in that fight has become a showpiece. With a massive political mobilization of the entire business community, employers were able to defeat a much-sought union proposal that was backed by the administration. The business lobbies were characterized by a high degree of organization and unity, very generous financing, and a heavy grass-roots response. As in the past, the business organizations were able to manipulate public opinion skillfully.

Although the fight over common situs picketing legislation was essentially a construction industry issue, the great majority of employer organizations were mobilized for the conflict. It provided a dry run in coalition-building and public information campaigning that stood business in good stead in the main event two years later. The unexpected victory by the employer community in the common situs fight gave business lobbyists a much-needed psychological boost. As a result, business launched a more vigorous offensive against labor law reform, which appeared to have altered the power relationship between business and labor interests in Washington.

Since 1978, there has been a virtual standoff between employer organizations and the union movement with respect to labor law. During its first two years, the Reagan administration shifted the balance of power in favor of business interests and made some significant administrative changes but made no attempt to change the law itself.

The Wagner Act

Declaring that collective bargaining is essential to avoid "industrial strife or unrest," the Wagner Act of 1935 authorized the formation of the National Labor Relations Board (NLRB) to administer the act's provisions. The heart of these provisions was section 7, which guaranteed workers the right to join labor organizations and the right "to bargain collectively through representatives of their own choosing. . . ." To secure these rights, the Wagner Act banned certain unfair labor practices by employers, the most basic of which was the interference with workers' rights guaranteed by section 7. Employers were also prohibited from discriminating against a worker on the basis of union membership in hiring or firing decisions, and from refusing to bargain collectively with the workers' authorized representatives.

Hailed as organized labor's Magna Carta, the Wagner Act represented a dramatic change in the federal government's policy towards labor-management relations. Early federal involvement took the form of judicial decrees or injunctions that employers could easily obtain to defeat any concerted activity by a union involved in a labor dispute. The injunction removed the symptoms of the dispute, usually a strike and picketing, but the underlying problem remained unresolved. Thus, the federal judiciary served merely to maintain the existing imbalance between employers and the fledgling unions.[1]

This policy was reversed by the Norris-LaGuardia Act in 1932, which established a laissez faire policy toward labor disputes by prohibiting the federal courts from issuing injunctions against union activities except in a few clearly defined cases. The Wagner Act once again put the federal government in the business of regulating labor-management relations. Rather than seeking to eradicate only the symptoms of labor unrest, however, the new legislation sought to insure industrial stability by promoting collective bargaining between employers and the representatives of their employees.

The First Four Decades

The Taft-Hartley Act

Employer associations were almost uniformly opposed to the Wagner Act. Not surprisingly, efforts were underway to modify significant portions of the act almost as soon as it was enacted. In the forefront of these efforts was the National Association of Manufacturers. Following passage of the Wagner Act, the NAM and other industry associations argued that the law was unconstitutional and brought suits seeking injunctions against enforcing NLRB rulings. When the Supreme Court upheld the constitutionality of the Wagner Act in April 1937, business shifted its strategy to seeking "equalizing" amendments to the labor laws to regulate union activity. Both the Chamber of Commerce and the NAM avoided endorsing collective bargaining even after leading employers had negotiated collective agreements. Although resigned to government's involvement in labor relations, the national employer associations found it a tough pill to swallow. The next phase of their lobbying activity, therefore, was directed not at seeking legislative repeal of the Wagner Act but at amending it to make government involvement more palatable.

In its fight to have the labor laws modified, the NAM initiated a long-range program to influence public opinion. It anonymously disseminated public educational materials such as cartoons, editorials, and news broadcasts. The material was widely used by employers to resist union organizational drives. The LaFollette Civil Liberties Committee publicized the antiunion campaigns of employers, and the impact of these activities on public opinion might have contributed to the failure of a business effort in 1938–39 to amend the act.

The war years brought a lull in the fight for labor law "equalization." However, early 1946 saw a resumption of the propaganda war. This time, the NAM and the Chamber were helped by the public's anger over the postwar strike wave. The employer associations seized the opportunity, labeling their proposals as being in the interest of individual employees and the public. Their well-organized campaign bore fruit in 1946 with the passage of the Taft-Hartley amendments establishing unfair labor practices by unions that paralleled unfair practices by employers, widening employers' access to the courts for injunctions, and permitting state right-to-work legislation (section 14(b)).

The Landrum-Griffin Act

Public opinion against organized labor following World War II, which culminated with the passage of Taft-Hartley, was revived at the end of the next decade when disclosures made by the McClellan Senate investigations committee linked several unions with organized crime. Employer groups sensed a favorable climate for the enactment of legislation regulating internal union affairs. Although the ostensible purpose of the legislation was to reduce the influence of racketeers in labor organizations, it was not a well-kept secret that such legislation was also aimed at weakening the power of unions in collective bargaining.

Employer association lobbyists followed a strategy similar to that which had proven successful in their Taft-Hartley campaign. Legitimate complaints against certain unions were selected and publicized widely. So successful was this public education campaign that even labor's supporters were forced to agree that legislation was needed to make unions disclose their financial activities, conduct democratic elections of union office-holders, and guarantee the rights of individual members.

Right-to-Work

Labor's failed attempt at repeal of Taft-Hartley's section 14(b) (which provided that states could enact right-to-work legislation prohibiting the union shop) is yet another example of the employer community's ability to win in Congress on union power issues. The liberal composition of the Eighty-ninth Congress offered organized labor an opportunity for repealing section 14(b). In the mid-1960s, many of the cornerstones of the Great Society were laid, and the union movement participated actively in the battles to get these programs enacted. Yet, when it came to realizing their own legislative priorities, even with the Johnson administration's help, the unions were frustrated. A bill repealing section 14(b) passed the House in the Eighty-ninth Congress but failed twice to overcome a filibuster in the Senate. A coalition of business groups, including the Chamber, the National Right-to-Work Committee, the NAM, and the Association for General Contractors effectively exploited the emotionalism of the issue. Employers hit hard on the arguments that repeal of 14(b) would violate individual worker freedoms and endow union leaders with excessive political power.

Business lobbies, as they had in the past, carried the day with a negative portrayal of the union movement, seizing on the image of the AFL-CIO as a political Goliath. The unions' arguments about the unfairness of "free riders" receiving union services and benefits without paying for them, the need for union security clauses to improve the quality of representation employees received, and the use of right-to-work laws by employers to sap union strength all paled in comparison with the image of a union power grab that business proponents of 14(b) were able to create.

It is significant that the unions' attempt at repealing 14(b) was followed closely by the formation of the Labor Law Study Group, a predecessor organization of the Business Roundtable. Since the mid-1960s, employers have managed to keep the repeal of 14(b) out of serious legislative consideration. In fact, recently they have even managed to drum up some support for a national right-to-work law.

Common Situs Picketing: A Surprise Win

By the 1970s, a pattern had emerged in legislative fights over union power issues. The employer groups succeeded in portraying theirs as the middle of the road position, painting unions and their supporters as selfish and intransigent. Using these tactics, business organizations have been able to best unions even when working with heavily Democratic Congresses, as in 1959 and 1965–66. Business has abandoned its opposition to government involvement in labor-management relations, choosing instead to influence the content of the nation's labor laws.

To retain the ban on common situs picketing, employer representatives effectively employed a broad-based coalition. Though of immediate consequence mainly to the construction industry, the controversy generated tremendous concern and activity across the business community. As major construction customers, business—particularly big business—had more than passing interest in the level of labor costs in construction. Business lobbyists also perceived the fight over situs picketing as a trial run for the scheduled battle over the pending omnibus labor law reform bill, the centerpiece of labor's agenda.

The issue at the center of the common situs debate is whether a construction trade union should have the right to picket a construction site when it has a dispute with the general contractor or a single subcontractor at the site. Since the passage of the Taft-Hartley Act and its interpretation by the Supreme Court in *National Labor Relations Board v. Denver Building and Construction Trades Council,* such an action has been considered illegal as a secondary boycott.

The unions have long argued that all they are seeking with a common situs provision is equality of picketing rights with industrial unions who have the power to shut down an entire manufacturing plant. In support of this argument, they maintain that all contractors and subcontractors on a site are engaged in a joint venture and, therefore, are not neutral employers in the disputes. Business, on the other hand, has argued that the individual contractors and subcontractors are independent employers and should, therefore, not be subject to collective action aimed at one of them. Employers also argue that legalizing common situs picketing would lead to more labor strife, an increase in construction costs, and a reduction of competition in the industry.

The significance of common situs picketing is its effectiveness as an organizing tool. With this in mind, unions have pressed repeatedly for congressional support of the legislation. As nonunion employers have made inroads on the construction industry, the legal status of situs picketing has become all the more important. By 1975, about 40 percent of the industry's gross volume was nonunion.

Victory by Veto—1975

Democrats scored significant victories in the first post-Watergate Congress. Counseled by Secretary of Labor John T. Dunlop, President Ford agreed to sign a common situs picketing bill if it contained provisions for changing the fragmented collective bargaining structure of the industry. To gain support for the fight against passage of the bill, the Associated General Contractors, the Associated Builders and Contractors, and their allies formed the National Action Committee on Secondary Boycotts. The Action Committee grew to include over a hundred business associations and corporations. In addition to about forty construction trade associations, it included the Chamber of Commerce, the NAM, the Business Roundtable, the National Federation of Independent Business, the National Small Business Association, the American Farm Bureau Federation, the American Retail Federation, the American Trucking Association, and the National Labor-Management Foundation. The coalition represented virtually all segments of the business community.

Though the Action Committee had a late start, it made up in intensity for the lost time. It sponsored a one-day "fly-in" of more than 700 executives from around the country to persuade representatives to vote against the bill. But the die was cast, and the House voted 230 to 178 in favor of the bill. Business lobbying succeeded in launching a filibuster against the bill in the Senate, which labor's allies eventually broke. In a last-ditch effort, the Action Committee organized a massive letter-writing campaign to persuade President Ford to veto the bill.[2] This "groundswell" was backed by personal visits from Roundtable members and contacts from other influential organization executives. Combined with pressure from Ford's rival for the 1976 Republican presidential nomination, Ronald Reagan, the work of the business lobby swayed President Ford to veto the bill, despite the objections of his Secretary of Labor, who subsequently resigned. The votes were not there to override the veto.

The organization assembled for the 1975 fight carried the day in the 1977 fight, too. Richard Creighton of the Associated General Contractors, who chaired the Action Committee, kept the core group of forty construction employer associations meeting weekly after the Ford veto in anticipation of a Democratic victory in the 1976 elections. When this materialized, the business coalition swung into action and expanded again to include seventy other organizations.[3] The employers were well prepared for labor's early initiative.

Victory by Persuasion—1977

When the 1976 elections put a Democrat in the White House and retained the Democratic majority in Congress, organized labor assumed that the chances for passage of a common situs picketing bill had improved in the Ninety-fifth Congress. President Carter promised to sign a common situs picketing bill, though he would not actively lobby for one. The unions, therefore, put the bill at the head of their legislative agenda on the assumption that its easy passage would pave the way for the other bills they favored, notably labor law reform. They also made the mistake of aiming the bulk of their lobbying efforts at the Senate, where they assumed they would meet the most opposition.

The employer community reasoned similarly. It saw the importance of breaking labor's stride early and also figured its best shot at stopping the bill was in the Senate. However, the National Action Committee on Secondary Boycotts decided not to write off the House and tried to make a good showing there as well. Business launched a sustained and massive lobbying effort in the House, including visits by local businessmen and waves of letters, telegrams, and telephone calls from constituents. It relied heavily on its highly mobilized grass roots.

The employer lobbies also undertook a major campaign to appeal to the general public. The burden of the effort was to portray the construction workers as already overpaid and greedy in demanding more, and the employers as the guardians of the public interest. The underlying idea was to persuade the public that the proposed situs picketing bill was the creation of grasping union bosses. "Who Wants Secondary Boycotts in Construction??? Not the American Public—Not Even Union Construction Workers!!!"[4]

The construction employers' campaign against common situs was notable for its use of the "rifle" strategy, in which business lobbyists carefully targeted members of Congress who they thought could be swayed to their side. The Action Committee concentrated on freshman House members and the approach paid off.

The unions had no trouble persuading the liberal House Education and Labor Committee to report out by a party line vote a common situs bill stronger than the one Ford had vetoed. However, as the floor vote on the bill neared, it became clear to labor's supporters that they did not have the votes. To woo broader support, the bill's Democratic sponsors agreed to a substitute bill sponsored by Ronald Sarasin of Connecticut, a moderate Republican on the Education and Labor Committee. The Sarasin compromise included broader exemptions from common situs picketing practices than had the committee bill; it was similar to the bill vetoed by Ford. Even additional last-minute compromises by the unions were not enough to save the measure from the business onslaught. On March 23, 1977 the House defeated the bill by a 217–205 vote. The outcome was almost as much of a surprise to the victors as it was to labor.

The employers' campaign against common situs was qualitatively different from anything that had been done previously—by them or by other groups. House Speaker Thomas P. O'Neill, Jr. commented that he had "never seen an organization function like the Associated General Contractors, the home builders, and the other" groups opposed to the picketing bill.[5] The battle was important to the business community because it showed what it could do against great odds when its lobbyists worked together. The employers' victory gave them a tremendous psychological boost because it reversed a string of business defeats in the early 1970s in occupational safety and health, consumer product safety, equal employment opportunity, pollution control, and private pension policy. Business profitably applied to the labor law reform fight the lessons it had learned in the common situs fight about coalition strategy and the value of a public relations campaign as a prelude to winning on the Hill. Had the business community lost common situs, it is quite likely it would have lost the battle over labor law reform, too.

Labor Law Reform: Pulling Out the Stops

The battle over labor law reform illustrated that a well-financed and well-coordinated campaign by the business community could overcome considerable odds and block the enactment of a major piece of legislation. The business community's victory in this battle was a showpiece of employer political prowess and represented a key turning point in the development of business's lobbying expertise in the 1970s. By stressing issues involving union power, the employer lobbies galvanized the entire business community to fight the bill.

Problems at the NLRB

Labor law reform in 1977 was aimed both at expediting various administrative and adjudicative functions of the NLRB and at strengthening the remedial provisions of the act in order to increase the deterrence to violation. A broad group of labor relations specialists, labor lawyers, and members of the board itself had long recognized the need for legislative modification in these two areas.

Contested NLRB proceedings have been characterized by long delays. Even in the mid-1970s, the median time elapsed from the filing of an unfair labor practice charge to the issuance of a board decision was nearly a year. Those cases needing enforcement of a board decision by a U.S. court of appeals take an additional year. Thus, from the filing of an unfair labor practice complaint to the enforcement of a NLRB order, an action can easily take two years or more. During this period, the aggrieved party has no remedy for the guilty party's wrongdoings. Fortunately, the board's regional offices have regularly settled approximately ninety-five percent of all charges filed. But the remaining cases are frequently the most important. In fiscal 1976, for example, over 1300 cases went before the board and the courts, and the number has steadily risen. Although the board has expedited successfully the handling of most unfair labor practice charges, action by the board or the court of appeals was needed more than twice as often in 1976 as in 1960. The board's statistics showed that, without some procedural changes, the situation would get worse before it got better. Indeed, this has been the case.

A potentially more serious problem has existed in representation cases, where a recalcitrant party can delay an election by arguing over frivolous issues, insisting on a hearing, and then filing postelection objections to delay certification of the results. Most elections held by the NLRB have the consent of both parties, and most election petitions are filed by unions or workers. Because unions contest employer petitions less often than employers contest union-sponsored petitions, the delay caused by the hearings is more frequently due to employer action and has tended to favor the management position.

In 1961, a House subcommittee held fifteen days of hearings on the problems caused by the board's procedures. Its report concluded that the labor board's orders were little more than "a slap on the wrist" and "a license fee for union busting" and recommended that remedies be fashioned to take the profit out of unfair labor practices.[6] That same year, President Kennedy failed to gain congressional approval of a board reorganization plan that would have expedited the procedures for handling unfair labor practices. Employer associations not only rallied against proposed changes in the substantive rights and duties of parties under the NLRA, but they also opposed procedural reforms intended to make the NLRB function more efficiently. Although seemingly committed in their public pronouncements to collective bargaining and freedom of choice for workers, the employer associations were not anxious for the NLRB to become too vigorous in implementing these principles.

The Bill

The labor law reform bill proposed many changes with origins in these early reports and recommendations. Most of the provisions were procedural in nature, though some did change the rights and duties of the parties under the law. Though the proponents claimed that the labor law reform bill was a modest piece of legislation, the opponents succeeded in presenting the proposal as another attempted union power grab.

The bill contained three provisions intended to speed the handling of unfair labor practice cases. First, it provided for a summary procedure whereby a panel of three board members would have the option of affirming an administrative law judge's decision, avoiding a complete hearing before the full NLRB. A second provision enlarged the size of the board from five to seven members, to reduce the workload on each member. Third, the bill expedited the enforcement of NLRB orders by the U.S. courts of appeals by legislating automatic enforcement of the board's decision if the losing party failed to appeal within thirty days.

Another set of three provisions would have altered the way the board handled representation cases. First, the bill required the board to promulgate regulations establishing types of employee units appropriate for collective bargaining. The NLRB currently decides this on a time-consuming, case-by-case basis. Utilizing rulemaking in addition to adjudicative procedures would have allowed the board flexibility in determining obviously appropriate units without resorting to hearings on each case. Second, the bill set forth an expedited timetable for the holding of elections. Third, the bill made provision for equal access to the employee group by union organizers and the employers.

The last category of provisions was supposed to discourage unfair labor practices by strengthening the remedies available to the victims. The remedies included multiple back pay formulas and the increased use of mandatory injunctions in cases of discriminatory discharge of employees for prounion sympathies, compensation for entire bargaining units in the event of an employer's refusal to bargain in good faith, and debarment from federal contracts in the cases of repeat or willful labor law violators.

The proposals eliciting the greatest controversy concerned the new procedures for representation elections, the equal access provision, and the increased penalties for labor law violators.

The Debate

The employer representatives put forward a unified front in their opposition to the proponents' arguments for labor law reform. A reasonably coherent employer position emerged from the debate, though there were differences in emphasis among the representatives of business organizations who testified against the bill.

The purpose of the proposal to enlarge the NLRB was to expedite the handling of unfair labor practice cases. The board operates under a modified panel system; each member chairs one panel and serves on two others. The panels hear cases and issue decisions under the board's imprimatur. However, each non–panel member reviews the decisions and can have the case referred to the full board for consideration. By adding two members, proponents reasoned, the board would be able to form more panels, and, therefore, hear more cases.

Opponents took issue with the above proposition, maintaining that board expansion would actually lengthen the delays. Since panel decisions must be cleared by all members, they argued, this provision would only increase the number of approvals needed and would therefore increase the number of cases the entire board would be required to consider.[7] Other management representatives were concerned that President Carter would pack the board with prolabor Democrats and that the newly composed board would issue grossly unfair decisions. A recent study of unfair labor practices has shown, however, that there is no evidence that unions win more cases under boards dominated by Democrats.[8]

The establishment of a summary affirmance procedure was intended to get around the board's awkward three-step decisionmaking process. Unfair labor practice cases are handled first by administrative law judges, second by the board in Washington, and third by the appropriate federal court of appeals. A great deal of duplication of effort is involved, especially in the first two stages. Employer representatives argued that the provision mandating a summary affirmance procedure would not expedite enforcement of board orders since it was already informal board practice to issue summary decisions in cases where a panel felt it was justified. Formalizing the procedure would only add one step to the decisionmaking process.

Opponents criticized the provision setting a time limit of thirty days for appeals of board decisions on the ground that it would result in more appeals, since there would be no time for voluntary compliance. The argument not only ignored the fact that a court of appeals is equipped to handle frivolous cases in a summary fashion but also overlooked the cost of the existing system to the aggrieved party. Since board orders are not self-enforcing, management can refuse to comply with an order even if it is found guilty of committing an unfair labor practice. The aggrieved party is without recourse until the court enforces the board's order, which may take months or even years. This delay is unreasonable, since the overwhelming majority of board decisions reaching the courts are ultimately enforced.

The proposed bill required that an election be held within fifteen days of the filing of the petition where a majority of the employees petition for a unit which is plainly appropriate under board rules; within seventy-five days, where an election presents exceptionally novel or complex issues; and within forty-five days in all other cases. The election timetable was included in the bill to reduce the opportunities available to either party to delay an election. The median time elapsed between the filing of a petition for an election and the holding of the election was seventy-five days when a preelection hearing was requested, but in some cases the delay was as much as one year.

The establishment of an election timetable was viewed by business as an attempt by unions to aid their lagging organizing drives. Workers, they argued, would be forced to vote before they heard the employer's position on the issue of unionization and before certain procedural problems, such as which employees were to be in the bargaining unit, were resolved. In fact, detailed study of representation elections found that when workers who had expressed an interest in joining a union at the beginning of a campaign changed their minds, it was rarely on account of greater familiarity with the company position.[9] The study concluded that what went on at the workplace before the organizational drive began was far more important than the employers' statements during the campaign in determining how the workers would vote.

The equal access provision was also controversial. Unlike most of the other provisions, it was substantive in nature, giving added rights to union organizers. Under present law, employers can require their workers to attend "captive audience" speeches and discuss, within certain limits, the disadvantages of unionization. Such privileges are not available to unions in presenting their position, and they often must depend upon discussions with individual workers in their homes or on handing out leaflets at the plant gate. The equal access provision would have allowed the organizer to address workers on company time and on company premises, if the employer chose to address the workers in that manner. Disregarding evidence that employers have distinct advantages under the current system, management representatives maintained that the effect of the proposals would be to silence employer communications and give unions an advantage in presenting their position to the employees. A more persuasive argument against the equal access provision was that it failed to consider the employer's property rights.

The primary reason for increasing the remedies available to the board under the NLRA was the increasing number of unfair labor practices. Within the decade prior to 1977, the year the labor reform bill was introduced, the number of unfair labor practice charges filed with the NLRB rose by 122 percent and the median number of unfair labor practice changes pending with the board was up 110 percent. Of the charges filed in fiscal 1977, 69 percent were alleged violations by employers, and of the complaints issued by the NLRB in that year, 83 percent were against employers.

Labor representatives sought to justify strengthening the remedies by bringing numerous victims of employer labor law violators to testify at the hearings. This tactic was similar to the use of horror stories of pension loss in the fight for ERISA. Management groups argued that the overwhelming majority of managements obey the law and that it is unfair to write laws for the many by generalizing from the experience of the few. Employers also objected to the strengthened remedies on the grounds that these provisions would change the act's nature from remedial to punitive.

The multiple back pay and the mandatory injunction provisions were both aimed at the problem of discriminatory discharge for prounion activities. The present remedy for an employee who is fired for union-related activity is reinstatement with back pay. This does not fully compensate the worker for any consequential losses incurred, nor does it provide adequate disincentive to the employer to fire the worker in the first place; a multiple back pay award would have done both. A discriminatory discharge has its greatest effect during an organizing campaign. By discharging an active prounion worker, the employer can intimidate the other employees from supporting the union. Under the current law, this interference with the employees' right of free choice remains unredressed. Mandating that the board seek an injunction against the discriminatory firing of a worker during an organizational drive or the negotiation of an initial collective agreement was intended to reduce the chilling effect of the firing on other workers who might want to support the union.

Employers' representatives took exception to the proposed remedies. The NAM objected to the multiple back pay remedy on the grounds that it would "encourage the lazy or ineffective worker to try to get discharged so he can seek the monetary rewards without even working."[10] However, this overlooked the fact that a fired employee would still have to prove that the dismissal was for engaging in protected concerted activity. The strengthened remedy would not have altered the basic question of fact that the board has to decide in such cases.

Employers also argued that mandatory injunctive relief should not apply to discriminatory discharge cases. Business justified restricting this mandatory remedy to unlawful union secondary boycotts or picketing by claiming that these violations involved a greater loss to the victims than a discriminatory discharge. Advocates of the proposal replied that victims of discriminatory discharges are rarely fully compensated and that injury to the individual in these situations is no less substantial or irreparable than in the cases currently covered by the mandatory injunction provision.

The "make-whole" remedy would have provided compensation to workers whose employer was found to have bargained in bad faith during negotiations for the initial contract. The labor reform bill would have authorized the board to compensate the employee group for the forgone wages and benefits and for the inability to have work-related grievances processed as through a negotiated agreement. Compensation would have been based on the percentage increase in wages and benefits received by unions reported by the Bureau of Labor Statistics. Employers suggested that under the proposed remedy, "a union representative would rather delay and hinder bargaining to catch the employer in one slip, and then let the board write the contract."[11] Supporters argued, however, that employer fears concerning the make-whole remedy were unfounded. They maintained that if a union tried to hinder bargaining, it would probably be found guilty of bargaining in bad faith.

The debarment remedy would have disqualified an employer found to be a willful labor law violator from receiving federal contracts for three years. Business representatives voiced the concern that employers who committed innocent violations of the NLRA would be subject to the provision. However, the House committee specified that only those employers who committed a voluntary, intentional violation of a known legal duty would be penalized.[12] In other words, more than mere negligence would have to be shown to invoke the bar. Another criticism directed at debarment was that it would hurt innocent employees. If a company were barred from receiving government contracts, its work force would presumably have to be reduced. Proponents conceded the possibility of some negative employment effects from this provision, but hoped that the severity of the remedy would deter employers from becoming subject to its penalty.

Employers objected most strenuously, then, to the provisions concerning representation election procedures and strengthened remedies. Business representatives opposed the bill on the grounds that by changing the rules of the game, it would give an unfair advantage to the unions in organizing campaigns. The NAM characterized the proposals as "a bag of free organizing tools for unions."[13] Labor acknowledged that the proposals would help organize large companies in the South that had been successful in avoiding unionization in the past.

Understandably, the unions tried to sell the bill for its symbolic value. The late AFL-CIO President George Meany declared that "the Labor Law Reform bill is a symbol of good faith. What happens to that symbol, in the Senate of the United States, will have a profound impact on the kind of labor-management relations that America will have in the years ahead."[14] Professor Quinn Mills apparently agreed when he characterized the labor law reform effort as essentially a moderate bill.[15]

Even if the probable consequences of the legislation did not warrant the effort made to defeat it, employer associations took a cue from the emphasis that organized labor placed on the bill. The unions were determined to regain the power on the national level to adjust labor laws to suit their ends. Business was just as adamant in its determination not to be outdone on Capitol Hill and to protect the status quo back at the plant or office.

Employer Mobilization

The lobbying battle over labor law reform was characterized by a considerable investment of resources, skillful organization, a major grass-roots campaign, highly financed media blitzes, and generous resort to hyperbole on both sides. Both unions and management had drawn lessons from their respective failures and victories in the common situs fight and had targeted their strategies accordingly.

The unions were determined not to be cast in the light of a "special interest" group going after a pet project. They emphasized, therefore, the social justice dimension of the issue rather than their institutional stake in it. The tone of the campaign was reflected in the comment by Thomas R. Donahue, then executive assistant to AFL-CIO President George Meany, claiming that the bill "is not an agenda to make unions strong, it's a program for people."[16] To make their case more convincing, the unions agreed to strike the controversial provisions calling for the repeal of section 14(b) of the Taft-Hartley Act. That was hardly a sacrifice, because President Carter had said that he would not work actively for a bill containing elimination of 14(b), though he would sign one.

To broaden the labor reform bill's base of support, the unions sought to form alliances with religious groups, minority representatives, and civil rights organizations. The AFL-CIO coordinated its legislative and public education campaign closely with the national consumer boycott of J.P. Stevens products spearheaded by the Amalgamated Clothing and Textile Workers. J.P. Stevens's history as a labor law violator was presented as a case study of how employers could use the nation's labor laws to frustrate the attempts of workers to organize. The unions made a concerted effort to portray their proposals as benefiting workers' rights in a fight against employers who violate the law, prompting the opponents of the bill to distance themselves from Stevens and label that textile manufacturer an aberration among employers.

The AFL-CIO formed a special task force headed by Victor Kamber, the research director for the AFL-CIO building and construction trades department, to work exclusively on its legislative agenda. The federation initially levied a special dues assessment amounting to $800,000 to finance its campaign. The unions later upped the ante to an estimated $2.5 million, still far below the presumed $5 million invested by the opposition in fighting the bill.

The employer lobbyists launched an intensive campaign to influence Capitol Hill, the general public, and their own grass roots. The command center of the campaign was the National Action Committee for Labor Law Reform, which was set up in June 1977. Creighton, who had masterminded the common situs effort, was one of three steering committee cochairpersons; the other two were Randolph Hale of the NAM and Harold Coxson of the Chamber. The NAC was a new organization, more broadly based than the group established to fight the common situs picketing legislation but patterned after it.

The heavyweights in the campaign were the Chamber, the NAM, the Roundtable, and the construction trade associations, but the small employers were also very active. One quite energetic participant, though not a formal member of the National Action Committee, was the National Right-to-Work

Committee. The Right-to-Work Committee alone spent between $1 and $2 million on direct mail efforts and newspaper advertising in the campaign. Its direct mail operation used the computerized mailing lists of New Right organizer Richard Viguerie. Reportedly, the Committee mailed fifty million cards to constituents, of which an estimated six million found their way back to Capitol Hill. The Right-to-Work Committee had been a *bona fide* member of the National Action Committee on Secondary Boycotts; its status as mere "observer" to the labor law reform action committee was not an accident. It reflected a conscious decision on the part of the NAC's organizers that, to succeed, the campaign had to avoid the pitfall of appearing to be directed against unionism *per se*.[17]

Big business was a very important participant in the fight against labor law reform, but it joined the battle late. The Business Roundtable was divided on whether to jump into the fray against the bill. The heavily unionized firms wanted to avoid extramural conflicts with their unions. Since the bill was aimed at organizing employers who had long resisted unionization, those who had a history of dealing with the labor movement did not feel particularly threatened by it. On the other hand, Sears Roebuck and Company argued forcefully in favor of taking a stand, as did Firestone, Goodyear, and Bethlehem Steel. When the Roundtable's policy committee voted in August 1977 to move actively against labor law reform, the potential compromisers lost by a 19–11 vote.[18]

The Roundtable then closed ranks with the Chamber, the NAM, and other organizations. The large corporations provided most of the funding for the effort. Big business financed the public relations work of Edie Fraser Associates, which commissioned public opinion polls, wrote canned editorials for placement in newspapers, and sent out reprints of favorable comments by the press on the employers' position. A study by Rinfret Associates on the bill's probable inflationary consequences was financed by Roundtable and NAM members, and some corporations, including Sears and Shell Oil, wrote to their shareholders and retired employees urging support of their positions. Several corporations made their company jets available for the "march" on Washington, and executives of many companies made a pilgrimage to Capitol Hill. The fact that major corporate officials, who employed a significant portion of a legislator's constituents, would take time to express their views in person had the desired effect.

Much of the legwork was done, however, by owners of small businesses. They were represented by 500 state and local chapters of groups from the National Federation of Independent Business, the National Small Business Association, the U.S. Chamber, the American Retail Federation, the National Restaurant Association, the National Machinery and Tooling Association, and others. These groups coordinated their efforts through a state chairperson in each of thirty-one targeted states. Using small business to carry the torch against labor law reform was an extremely effective tactic. Supporting small business interests generally gets higher marks with constituents than supporting the interests of big business. James McKevitt of the NFIB boasted, "They're riding our coattails, not vice versa."[19] Ironically, many small business owners did not meet the NLRB's minimum jurisdictional dollar level and therefore were not directly affected by the agency. Addressing the annual meeting of the Chamber in May 1978, Senator Orrin Hatch of Utah argued that the bill "in many ways could make a difference whether small business survives in this country."[20] The unions had perceived the bill as aiding their drive against the large employers resisting unionization in the South and were not well prepared to meet the assault of small employers.

Of course, the grass-roots strategy did not rely entirely on the small business community. Much of the organization was derived from the computerized membership lists of the National Right-to-Work Committee, the Association of General Contractors, and the Chamber. The Chamber's congressional action committees, the AGC's legislative network, and comparable systems of other organizations played important roles. The product was a virtual blitzkrieg on Capitol Hill.

The purpose of the NAC's grass-roots strategy was to shatter the appearance of a broad consensus behind labor law reform. A presumably confidential NAM memorandum described this strategy:

> we should try to make [labor law reform] an issue that would be 'too hot to handle.' We should emphasize that the proposed legislation has already aroused the wrath of the entire business community, and that any showdown on the bill will be far more than anything Congress has seen in a long while. In this vein, individual member companies should be encouraged to contact their Representatives early and vent their horror.[21]

The business lobbyists apparently succeeded in making the issue "too hot to handle." In fact, their effort was so extensive that it suffered from overkill. For example, Senator Lawton Chiles of Florida was so besieged by employers from the hotel, restaurant, and resort industries concerned that the bill would lead to the unionization of their low-paid employees that he had to call a halt. An aide to the Senator said, "They were all set to haul up another couple of planeloads. The Senator had to tell them not to bother. There just wasn't any further point."[22]

This massive grass-roots lobbying effort was aimed at isolating labor by portraying the reform bill as a union power grab at the expense of employers and their employees. A key element of this strategy was the introduction of an alternative bill by the employer coalition called the "Employee Bill of Rights."

The employer strategy was to dispel the idea that business was against *any* reform and to make it appear that employers, rather than unions, had the best interests of individual employees in mind.[23]

Introduced by Representative John Erlenborn of Illinois and Senator Orrin Hatch, the bill was based on legislative proposals drawn up under the auspices of the Labor Law Study Group in the late 1960s. The main provisions of the Employee Bill of Rights included: (1) the right of the employer or ten percent of the employees to request a secret ballot to vote on union representation and strikes; (2) a ban on union-imposed fines of members who violate certain union rules or file decertification petitions; (3) the broadening of the permissible arguments employers could make during an organizing campaign; (4) a prohibition on union contributions to state and local elections and on the use of the dues check-off for political purposes; and (5) a ban on forcing individuals to join a union if they are opposed to such membership on religious grounds.[24]

Much of the Employee Bill of Rights was concerned with regulating the internal affairs of unions. Administration and labor opponents of the proposals argued that the Landrum-Griffin Act already addressed the alleged abuses the Erlenborn-Hatch bill focused on. Further legislation, they claimed, was unnecessary. Though employer representatives all endorsed the bill in their testimony, they didn't push for its enactment. The main purpose of the bill was to blunt labor's drive by shifting the focus of the discussion of labor law reform from questions of collective rights to individual worker rights, and in this it was moderately successful.

The Battle in Congress

Labor and its supporters had the jump on employers in the early stages of the labor law reform battle in the House. The opening salvo was launched by Representative Frank Thompson of New Jersey early in 1977 when he introduced HR77. After President Carter sent his proposals for NLRB reform to Congress in July 1977, they were introduced by Congressman Thompson (HR 8410) and Senators Harrison Williams of New Jersey and Jacob Javits of New York (S1883). A somewhat optimistic goal was to have the labor reform bill through both houses by Christmas.

With a two-to-one majority on the House Education and Labor Committee, Democrats had no trouble defeating the Employee Bill of Rights and approving the Thompson-sponsored labor reform bill by a voice vote on 22 September 1977. HR8410 was debated for three days on the House floor two weeks later. The employer associations' intended strategy in the House was to introduce dozens of weakening amendments to the Thompson bill. However, the bill's supporters pushed through a procedural measure which allowed amendments only to those portions of the NLRA which the Thompson bill amended. Most of the amendments which the bill's opponents managed to bring to the floor were voted down anyway. Those that succeeded had the support of the bill's floor managers and did not change it substantially. The House approved the labor reform bill by a comfortable 257 to 163 vote.

Employer spokespersons were highly critical of the procedure by which labor law reform was considered by the House. A spokesman for the NAC commented on the ''startling speed'' with which the unions got the measure through the House and called its passage ''the most outrageous demonstration of unchecked union power ever witnessed on Capitol Hill.''[25] The main reason for the remarkably quick passage in the House was that the employers had yet to crank up their grass-roots campaign and so were hard put to apply real pressure on vulnerable House members. Labor, on the other hand, had been extremely well organized from the start; the unions had learned their lesson from the defeat of the common situs picketing bill and didn't want to leave anything to chance in this round. Moreover, they were working with a clear Democratic majority in the House and a supportive administration. Furthermore, because business had yet to rev up its public relations machine, the House members viewed the bill as essentially a modest measure.

Following defeat in the House, the lobbyists representing the employer associations informally offered a compromise position on 2 December 1977:

— An election time limit of 45 days for all elections except those presenting novel or unusual legal questions, where a 75-day deadline might be appropriate;
— Elimination of the equal access provision;
— Double back pay awards, but with reduction for outside earnings;
— Contract debarment limited to specific locations of willful or flagrant unfair labor practices;
— Elimination of mandated wage and benefit increases based on BLS index of large units as a remedy for refusal to bargain;
— Expansion of board to seven members and establishment of summary affirmance procedure for ALJ decisions.

The proposal was rejected and never presented formally; the employers mobilized their resources and launched the full force of their campaign in the Senate. They knew that labor had the votes to pass the bill, so they mapped out a three-pronged strategy. First, they would try to defeat the bill by filibuster. Second, if the filibuster was broken, they would offer numerous crippling amendments to force a compromise. Third, if the amendments strategy didn't work, they planned to filibuster when the conference bill came up for consideration. They didn't have to go that far.

In January 1978, while the labor law reform bill was in committee, employer representatives were ready to compromise, but labor and its supporters were not interested. The unions counted sixty-two votes in support of their bill, and they only needed sixty to break a filibuster. Nonetheless, business was able to win a few concessions involving employee compensation in cases of unfair labor practices committed by employers and involving the procedures for accelerating union representation elections. Business also managed to get the religious objector clause of the Employee Bill of Rights incorporated into the bill. The full committee reported the bill to the floor on January 25 by a vote of thirteen to two. Senate action on the bill was delayed, however, until mid-May because the administration pressed the Senate to consider the Panama Canal treaties before labor law reform. The delay gave NAC time to flood the Senate with eight million pieces of mail, lobby more senators, take out more advertisements, and publish more expert studies on the allegedly dire impact of the bill. The vote on the Canal treaties probably worked to the employers' advantage, because it placed pressure on some senators not to cast a "liberal" vote on two controversial bills in a row. The 110-day strike by the United Mine Workers (from December 1977 through March 1978) could not have hurt the employers' cause, either.

In January, the unions probably had the votes they needed to invoke cloture on the employers' filibuster, but not four months later. The Senate debate occupied nineteen days between May 16 and June 22. Senator Javits criticized business's "campaign of blatant misrepresentation," Senator Hatch in turn called it a "blatant union power grab," and Senator Helms railed against "push-button" unionism.[26] In short, it was a lively debate. Six attempts were made to invoke cloture, all falling short of the needed sixty votes. Labor's allies got as many as fifty-eight votes on two attempts. The lobbying efforts of the small business owners were crucial in preventing several wavering senators from voting for cloture.

After a compromise bill put forward by Senate Majority Leader Robert Byrd of West Virginia and supported by the labor reform bill's original sponsors was rejected, the Democratic leadership finally had the bill recommitted to the Committee on Labor and Human Resources. Senator Williams' attempt to put together a package acceptable to the opponents of the bill also failed because the employer representatives were not interested in a compromise, believing that they had succeeded in stopping the sought labor reforms. On September 29, 1978 the Senate Subcommittee on Labor decided to postpone markup indefinitely for the "bare bones" proposal.

So business won. The employers' victory was the product of a combination of circumstances. Clearly, unions could not match the massive resources invested in the battle by business groups and individual corporations. It was not only a matter of finances, however. The scope of the employer mobilization and the degree to which different segments of the business community were able to work together and build a winning coalition were probably the most important aspects of the campaign. Also, business succeeded in capturing the political center by portraying the issue as a union power grab and the union movement as greedy. In particular, the elevation of the small businessman to the exalted position of potential victim of big labor—even though the bill's impact on small business would have been minimal—was a skillful exploitation of a key American value. Supporting small business plays well in every state and congressional district. Finally, the delay in the Senate vote as a result of the Panama Canal treaty controversy was a fortunate event for business. It allowed the NAC to make up for its slow start in the beginning of the campaign, and it strengthened the resistance of some senators to voting with labor on the reform bill.

Labor-Management Standoff

The labor law reform bill has not been reintroduced since 1978. Common situs picketing has been a dead issue, too. In fact, since the battle over labor law reform, issues of union power have had a relatively low profile in Congress. Even in the first two years of the Reagan administration, and with the changed composition of the Ninety-seventh Congress, neither side has had the votes or the will to push through a bill that would significantly alter the existing rules controlling industrial relations. The situation has remained unchanged in the Ninety-eighth Congress.

A number of reasons account for the lack of movement on labor law reform issues. Most important has been the low priority accorded to labor law issues by the Reagan administration. Controversy over budget and tax cuts dominated the first session of the Ninety-seventh Congress, and inflation and rising unemployment took center stage in the 1982 election year. Second, even if the Reagan administration tried to sponsor antiunion legislation, its chances of success are far from clear. Given that liberals would keep any legislative attack on union power bottled up in committee in the House, it has seemed politically prudent to avoid controversial union power issues that could hurt the chances for passage of other, higher-priority legislation. The 1982 elections further lessened chances of antiunion legislation in the House. Even in the Senate Committee on Labor and Human Resources, Republican moderates were likely to defect to the Democratic side when it came to polarized labor-management votes; it happened in connection with the nomination of John van de Water, a management consultant, for membership on the NLRB.

The labor law battles of the 1970s, then, have shown the business community what it can do when it sticks together and when employer representatives do their homework. The labor law reform battle and the common situs picketing fight were notable for the scale of coalition-building involved in the employer effort to defeat both bills. Both fights were won against considerable odds. The labor law reform fight was a showpiece of business's political prowess. Employers were united in their policy positions on the bill and mobilized grass-roots support for their lobbying efforts. Excellent organization, generous financing, and an expert use of the media were all key ingredients in the employer success. As in previous labor law fights, business was able to portray the union movement in a negative light and thereby capture the political center. The championing of the Employee Bill of Rights, focusing on the protection of individual rights as a legislative alternative to the labor law reform bill, lent credence to the claims of employers that they had the true interests of employees at heart.

The employer community also made an astute tactical judgment in playing up the presumed interests of the small business community in labor law reform. This reflected a recognition among employers that backing big business can be a political liability for legislators, whereas supporting the smalls plays well in Peoria.

Despite the essential modesty of the provisions of the labor law reform bill, the employer and union campaigns were remarkable for their intensity. As has been demonstrated in previous legislative battles, union power issues evoke an emotionalism that is unique. By making the issue one of a union power grab, employers were able to use the specter that the bill would enhance the power of unions and threaten the rights of individual employees and employers.

8

Lobbying Lessons

The three case studies strongly suggest that the business lobbyists have learned some important lessons about the rules of the game. Business representatives have recognized the importance of doing their homework and offering positive policy alternatives—objection to government regulation in principle is not enough. The employers' position and actions on the Employee Retirement Income Security Act (ERISA) debate offer a prime illustration. With more positive alternatives to those proposed by the supporters of pension regulations, the business community might have been more successful in fending off the onslaught of government intrusion. Their arguments against the proposals for a mandatory universal pension system in the late 1970s demonstrated an emphasis on alternative ways of expanding coverage. Whether or not the arguments are viable is often less important politically than the impression they give of the employer community's concern over the social goals to be addressed. The cuts that were made in unemployment insurance in the Omnibus Reconciliation Act of 1981, although detrimental for the unemployed, were presented in a coherent fashion by the business lobbyists as good for the UI system and, incidentally, good for the economy. Similarly, the employer lobbies' use of the Employee Bill of Rights in the labor law reform fight demonstrated that making popularly appealing alternative proposals—even if they are not seriously considered by legislators—strengthens a campaign by making opposition appear to be more than naysaying.

Business lobbies are learning to attractively package proposals that serve their self-interest and to market their agendas more successfully to the public. It is not sufficient to cry "Cost!" or raise the specter of socialism—now business must make the public believe that the public interest coincides with that of business. George P. Shultz, in describing his experience with employer representatives during the Nixon administration, brought home this point:

> Many came in very poorly prepared, with only general complaints and
> groans and without real substance to back up their points or practical
> suggestions for dealing with them. Many of these petitioners probably

went away feeling that I was unresponsive and unsympathetic. Increasingly, however, it seemed to me that businessmen were learning that homework pays off. This is not simply a matter of being factually informed and reasonably objective in presentation. It also means looking beyond the very narrow interests of the individual firm or industry and offering some connection between what you want and broader public interest.[1]

The employer organizations have realized that many of the same techniques apply to politics and business. The marketing techniques and packaging of legislative proposals may differ from efforts to sell beer or soap, but the need to apply marketing principles is no less important.

A second very important lesson the business community has learned is that success in Washington involves constant vigilance and political intelligence. Once something is given away on Capitol Hill, it is difficult to get it back. The experience with federal regulation of private pensions offers an excellent lesson. Employer representatives were slow to react to proposed pension legislation, and Congress passed the Employee Retirement Income Security Act over strong employer objections. Despite the many problems connected with ERISA, employer lobbies have not succeeded in changing the shortcomings of the law by 1983—nine years after the passage of the legislation. Surely, nothing as costly as ERISA could again move through Congress without employer representatives' being carefully prepared for it. On the other hand, the employer community avoided giving away the store in the case of unemployment insurance. Business has been on top of developments in UI at the federal as well as the state levels. Though employers lost considerable ground in the mid-1970s, they have managed by and large to control the program during its nearly five decades. In the labor law battles, employers lost big in 1935 but have managed since then to win every significant encounter by adroit and timely manipulation of public sentiment against excessive union power, as the conflicts during the 1970s over common situs and labor law reform demonstrate.

Perhaps the most important lobbying lesson the employer community has learned is that a united front is normally a necessary condition for success. Business unity has been proven time and again to be the most important ingredient for success in legislative campaigns. Clearly, in unity there is strength, but employer organizations are no monolith, and conflicts of interest are frequently unavoidable. Lack of unity on key pension issues proved costly to employers. The divisions between big and small employers and between single employer and multiemployer pension plans have been significant handicaps to united business community lobbying on pension issues. The controversy over the restructuring of the pension plan termination insurance program has particularly exacerbated the conflict between sponsors of single employer and multiemployer plans. The two groups of sponsors reached an agreement that formed part of the foundation for the 1980 amendments to the 1974 pension law, but it has broken down after the fact. A newly fashioned coalition will be needed if business lobbyists are to push through any more of their desired ERISA reforms. The divisions between big and small can, however, be patched over by skillful compromise, as they have been to some degree by large employers' efforts to support small employers' grievances regarding costs of paperwork and "overregulation." This piggybacking of big business on the smalls was also prominent in the arguments trotted out against labor law reform.

Business has had an easier time maintaining a united front in the UI field, straddling the divisions between low-wage and high-wage employers when it comes to financing issues. In the labor law area, the division between employers whose companies are organized and those who are "union-free" is significant but has proven surmountable. In the early stages of the labor law reform controversy, the uneven commitment to launching an all-out fight was evidenced in the divisions within the Business Roundtable. However, the symbolism of the union power issue eventually caught up most of the employer community in the campaign. In this case, ideology took precedence over economics. This has been taken as an indication by some union leaders that, "deep down," even some employers accustomed to dealing with unions have never really accepted unionism.

Coalition-building within the employer community, then, has proven easier in some areas than others. Considering the conflicts of interest among various employer groups, unanimity is frequently difficult to achieve, but it is normally needed to win legislative battles on broad issues. The coalition-building technique was successfully employed on a large scale in the 1975 and 1977 fights against labor law reform. Significantly, the labor law campaign got off to a slow start in 1977 because of squabbling among the main associations as to which organization would head the collective effort.

In the unemployment insurance area, business lobbies have presented a united front for many years and it has paid off most handsomely and repeatedly in the fight against federalization of the UI system. Experience has shown the desirability of establishing a central coordinating body to direct lobbying efforts, carry out continuous political intelligence, and conduct research. Such an organization exists on a permanent basis in the UI field—UBA, Inc.—and it appears to have been a very good investment over the years for the business community.

Much of the coordination that takes place among employer associations on various issues is informal. Ad hoc groups are formed by staff members of the organizations with a direct stake in an issue that is on the legislative horizon. They exchange information and, when appropriate, plan strategy on particular bills. The membership of these groups may change, but the activities are a crucial part of the Washington operation of every trade association executive and day-to-day corporate representative. Because of the extent of its resources, the Chamber is often at the center of these groups. In 1982, it listed over sixty "issue strategy groups" in which it was a participant. In the labor field these included the Washington industrial relations coordinating committee, Washington OSHA group, unemployment compensation strategy group, ERISA breakfast group, benefits overview group, ad hoc immigration reform group, employment and training strategy group, prevailing wage reform group, social security strategy group, and the Washington equal employment opportunity group. The national action committees on the common situs and labor law reform conflicts were major examples of ad hoc groups. They were tremendously helpful in the effort to coordinate the direct lobbying and grass-roots efforts of hundreds of independent employer organizations.

Coalition-building is essential because competition for the attention of legislators is very intense. As governmental regulation has expanded, so has the number of affected interests. Employers now need a credible vehicle to organize a broad cross-section of business (and other) interests to persuade policymakers in Congress and executive agencies that an issue deserves their attention and action.

The political affiliation of the White House occupant is important to the success of business lobbyists' legislative campaigns, but the orientation of public opinion on a particular issue can be crucial. ERISA was signed by a Republican president and the expansion of the UI system in the mid-1970s also took place during a Republican administration, whereas the defeat of labor law reform came during a Democratic administration which owed a political debt to the labor movement. These examples illustrate that although business is unable to shift public opinion on demand, it is quite capable of capitalizing on public sentiment favorable to its own point of view to achieve its legislative goals. Over the years, the employer lobbyists have been quite skillful at molding public opinion on questions of union power. By playing on the American public's fear of threats to individual rights and by using public information campaigns to portray the power of unions to call strikes affecting the national economy, business has won the major labor law battles since the passage of the Wagner Act. At the other extreme, business lobbies have made no inroads on public opinion in the case of pension legislation. The public has placed guaranteeing retirement income above any reservations it may have had about government intervention in business affairs.

In the first two years of the Reagan administration, macroeconomic policy issues predominated. The rise of unemployment above the ten percent mark shifted public attention to microeconomic policies dealing with job creation. As the recession deepened and the federal deficit kept on rising, business leaders lost whatever confidence they had in supply side economics and their support of Reaganomics wavered. Based on his interviews with business executives, pollster Louis Harris concluded that "supply side . . . is finally dead."[2] The Reagan administration did not come up with clear-cut alternatives; business leaders were left with the hope that economic recovery will reduce the federal deficit, but without an agenda.

Whatever unity business lobbies forged in 1981 clearly broke down in 1982 and might disintegrate in the years ahead. In 1981, "business tended to back the President, right or wrong. . . . the blind loyalty of 1981 is gone forever," according to Jack Carlson, executive vice president of the largest trade organization, the National Association of Realtors.[3]

Having gotten all they could have wanted in 1981 and given up some in 1982, business lobbyists may turn their attention to labor and related issues in 1983. That the Reagan administration will embrace these issues and that Congress will be responsive to business lobbies' pressures if they turn in that direction remained doubtful as the Ninety-eighth Congress, which opened for business on January 3, 1983, wrestled with unprecedented high deficits and the highest unemployment levels since the Great Depression.

Many, if not most, business leaders have found it difficult to adjust to the welfare state, but simplistic supply side solutions have proven to be no working substitute. The business community has made great strides in exerting its influence when it has been able to forge coalitions with the vast majority of the American body politic. Senate majority leader Howard Baker called the policy decisions of 1981 a "river-boat gamble." The business community can play a very productive role in altering the course of public policy before the river boat founders on the shoals.

If supply side economics is dead, then the business community will have to devise a new view of how the world works and chart its future course accordingly. Foreign models of government-industry-labor cooperation and aid are often pictured. Yet only one side of the foreign two-way street is most often displayed. It is not just what foreign corporations get from government and industry; of equal importance is what industry leaders are willing to give in terms of a social commitment.

The American economy now faces grave problems, including high unemployment, market competition from abroad, and arrested growth in productivity at home. Past economic advances in America have required the active participation of the government as well as broad public support. Such combined efforts and social partnerships have a strong tradition in the American fabric. A pioneer advocate of expanding American industry, Alexander Hamilton, noted that business "may be beneficially stimulated by prudent aids and encouragements on the part of government." This remains true today.

But this leads inexorably back to Adam Smith's observations that opened this study. Business always has had a serious image problem, as even the worldly philosopher of the invisible hand recognized. The occasional lack of social responsibility on the part of certain segments of industry has not helped this image problem. Any realistic policy to boost America's faltering productivity, capital formation, and economic development will require a positive governmental role. The challenge for business is to cooperate with the government and other sectors of the American economy in order to assure that the new policies are implemented with due regard for equity and fairness to all the partners in the economy.

Notes

Chapter 1

1. Wesley C. Mitchell, *Lecture Notes on Types of Economic Theory* (New York: Augustus M. Kelley, 1949), 1: 11–14.

2. Irving S. Shapiro, "Business and the Public Policy Process," in *Business and Public Policy,* ed. John T. Dunlop (Cambridge: Harvard University Press, 1980), pp. 28–29.

3. Kim McQuaid, "The Roundtable: Getting Results in Washington," *Harvard Business Review,* May-June 1981, p. 118.

4. Norman J. Ornstein and Shirley Elder, *Interest Groups, Lobbying, and Policymaking* (Washington, D.C.: Congressional Quarterly Press, 1978), pp. 80–82.

5. T. S. Ashton, *The Industrial Revolution: 1760–1830* (London: Oxford University Press, 1972), pp. 88–89.

6. *The Federalist Papers* (New York: New American Library, 1961), Essay No. 10, p. 80.

7. Sidney Fine, *Laissez Faire and the General Welfare State* (Ann Arbor: University of Michigan Press, 1976), pp. 111, 139.

8. Richard Hofstadter et al., *The Structure of American History* (Englewood Cliffs, N.J.: Prentice-Hall, 1973), pp. 275–76, 281.

9. Arthur F. Bentley, *The Process of Government* (San Antonio, Texas: Principia Press, 1949), p. 455.

10. David B. Truman, *The Government Process* (New York: Alfred A. Knopf, 1971), p. 18.

11. James M. Buchanan and Gordon Tullock, *The Calculus of Consent* (Ann Arbor: University of Michigan Press, 1971), p. 290.

12. L. R. Boulware, "Politics—the Businessman's Biggest Job in 1958," *Labor Law Journal,* August 1958, p. 581.

13. Ornstein and Elder, *Interest Groups,* pp. 14–17; and Theodore J. Lowi, *The End of Liberalism* (New York: W. W. Norton and Co., 1979), p. 67.

14. Elizabeth Drew, "Politics and Money," *The New Yorker,* December 6, 1982, pp. 54–149; and ibid., December 13, 1982, pp. 57–111.

Chapter 2

1. Philip H. Burch, Jr., "The NAM as an Interest Group," *Politics and Society,* Fall 1973, p. 102.

2. Andrew J. Glass, "NAM's New Look Is Toward Goal of Business Unity," *National Journal,* January 5, 1974, p. 17.

3. Karen DeW. Lewis, "NAM Turns Pragmatic in Opposing Federal Restraints on Industry," *National Journal,* June 3, 1972, p. 940.

4. Richard W. Gable, "NAM Influential Lobby or Kiss of Death?" *Journal of Politics,* May 1953, pp. 254–73.

5. "NAM Is Playing by a New Set of Rules," *Business Week,* December 17, 1966, pp. 116, 118.

6. NAM, Board of Directors, "Policy Position on Retirement Security," October 15–17, 1982, p. 7.

7. Robert S. Greenberger, "Manufacturers' Lobby Alters Style to Combat Its Obstructionist Image," *Wall Street Journal,* May 5, 1981, p. 1.

8. Robert Wiebe, *Businessmen and Reform: A Study of the Progressive Movement* (Chicago: Quadrangle Books, 1962), p. 33.

9. Cited in Mark Green and Andrew Buchsbaum, *The Corporate Lobbies: Political Profiles of the Business Roundtable and the Chamber of Commerce* (Washington, D.C.: Public Citizen, 1980), p. 23.

10. Timothy D. Schellhardt, "Chamber of Commerce Showdown Looms After Split on Taxes," *Wall Street Journal*, August 30, 1982, p. 15.

11. John F. Berry, "U.S. Chamber Unlikely Scene of Feud over Power, Politics," *Washington Post*, November 15, 1982, pp. 1, 5.

12. Robert T. Gray, "A New Day in Court for Business," *Nation's Business*, August 1978, p. 28.

13. Patricia Goldman, "US Chamber Works to Erase Negative Image and Improve Grassroots Clout," *National Journal*, April 1, 1972, p. 559.

14. Richard I. Kirkland, Jr., "Fat Days for the Chamber of Commerce," *Fortune*, September 21, 1981, p. 156.

15. "The Last Word in Business Communication," *Nation's Business*, October 1982, p. 34.

16. Suzanne Garment, "Wired Elections: Technology War for the Candidate," *Wall Street Journal*, December 24, 1982, p. 4.

17. Daniel Balz, "The Chamber and the NAM—A Marriage of Convenience," *National Journal*, August 7, 1976, p. 1105.

18. "Business Lobbyists Blend Their Voices," *Business Week*, June 21, 1976, p. 31.

19. G. William Domhoff, *The Powers That Be* (New York: Vintage Books, 1979), p. 118.

Chapter 3

1. Edward A. Filene, "What Business Men Think: See the New Deal Through," *Nation*, December 9, 1934, pp. 707–9.

2. Gerald R. Rosen, "Who Speaks for Business?" *Dun's Review*, November 1969, p. 47.

3. Broadus Mitchell, *Depression Decade: From New Era Through New Deal: 1929–1941* (New York: Holt, Rhinehart, and Winston, 1962), pp. 242–44, 284; and Murray Edelman, "New Deal Sensitivity to Labor Interests," in *Labor and New Deal*, ed. Milton Derber and Edwin Young (Madison: University of Wisconsin Press, 1957), p. 170.

4. Stanley Marcuss, as quoted in Dunlop, *Business and Public Policy*, pp. 103–4.

5. Derek C. Bok and John T. Dunlop, *Labor and the American Community* (New York: Simon and Schuster, 1970), pp. 27–28.

6. Robert M. Collins, "Positive Business Responses to the New Deal: The Roots of the Committee for Economic Development, 1933–42," *Business History Review*, Autumn 1978, p. 371.

7. Gerald R. Rosen, "Business' Most Powerful Club," *Dun's Review*, December 1976, p. 70.

8. Green and Buchsbaum, *The Corporate Lobbies*, p. 83.

9. Interview with Robert Holland, President, Committee for Economic Development, Washington, D.C., December 15, 1982.

10. William C. Frederick, "Free Market vs. Social Responsibility: Decision Time at the CED," *California Management Review*, Spring 1981, pp. 20–28.

11. Committee for Economic Development, *Public-Private Partnership* (New York: The Committee, February 1982), p. 80.

12. *National Labor Policy*, prepared by an independent study group (New York: Committee for Economic Development, 1961).

13. Peter Slavin, "The Business Roundtable: New Lobbying Arm of Big Business," *Business and Society Review*, Winter 1975–76, p. 29.

14. McQuaid, "The Roundtable," p. 118.

15. Philip H. Burch, "The Business Roundtable: Its Make-Up and External Ties" in *Research in Political Economy,* ed. Paul Zarembka (Greenwich, Conn.: JAI Press, 1981), IV: 104.

16. Cited in Haynes Johnson and Nick Kotz, *The Unions,* A *Washington Post* National Report (New York: Pocket Books, 1972), p. 115.

17. Albro Martin, letter to the editor, *Harvard Business Review,* July-August 1981, p. 170.

18. Richard E. Cohen, "The Business Lobby Discovers That in Unity There Is Strength," *National Journal,* June 28, 1980, p. 1052.

19. "The Swarming Lobbyists," *Time,* August 7, 1978, p. 17.

20. National Small Business Association, "The Small Business Legislative Council" (pamphlet).

21. Brigette Rousen, "Small Business Lobbying with National Organizations: More People Are Listening," *Congressional Quarterly Weekly Report,* March 1, 1980, pp. 609–16.

22. Sandra S. Bower, "Watch Out Washington, Here Come the Trade Associations," *National Journal,* June 9, 1979, p. 956; and Sandra Teeley, "Trade Associations," *Washington Post,* January 31, 1983, p. B1.

23. Carol S. Greenwald, *Group Power, Lobbying, and Public Policy* (New York: Praeger Publishers, 1977), p. 201.

24. Gilbert Burck, "A Time of Reckoning for the Building Unions," *Fortune,* June 4, 1979, pp. 83–84.

25. Don Bonafede, "Issue-Oriented Heritage Foundation Hitches Its Wagon to Reagan's Star," *National Journal,* March 20, 1982, p. 503.

Chapter 4

1. Shapiro, "Public Policy Process," p. 30.

2. Interview with Norman Ornstein, fellow, American Enterprise Institute for Public Policy Research, Washington, D.C., April 23, 1982.

3. Chamber of Commerce of the United States, *Washington Report,* September 1982.

4. Paul Taylor, "Chamber of Commerce Says Nay to Democrats," *Washington Post,* October 7, 1982, p. A10.

5. Interview with Herbert Liebenson, President, National Small Business Association, Washington, D.C., April 13, 1982.

6. Theodore H. White, *The Making of the President, 1964* (New York: Atheneum, 1965), p. 71.

7. Cited in Committee for Economic Development, *Public-Private Partnership,* p. 81.

8. Sidney Blumenthal, "Whose Side Is Business On, Anyway?" *New York Times Magazine,* October 25, 1981, pp. 20–31.

9. American Iron and Steel Institute, *Steel at the Crossroads: The American Steel Industry in the 1980s* (Washington, D.C.: The Institute, 1980), p. 14.

10. F. M. Scherer, *Industrial Market Structure and Economic Performance* (Chicago: Rand McNally Publishing Company, 1980), pp. 178–79.

11. William J. Lanouette, "Business Lobbyists Hope Their Unity on the Tax Bill Wasn't Just a Fluke," *National Journal,* October 24, 1981, p. 1898.

12. Bill Keller, "Dividing the Spoils: Democrats and Republicans Try to Outbid Each Other in Cutting Taxes for Business," *Congressional Quarterly,* June 17, 1981, pp. 1132–36.

13. William Greider, "The Education of David Stockman," *Atlantic,* December 1981, reprinted in *Congressional Record* (daily edition), November 10, 1981, p. S.13224.

14. Ibid.

15. Richard I. Kirkland, Jr., "In the Age of Ron, Celebrity Lobbies Are Losing the Limelight," *Fortune,* September 21, 1981, p. 156.

16. Timothy D. Schellhardt, "Chamber of Commerce Showdown Looms After Split on Tax Increases," *Wall Street Journal*, August 30, 1982, p. 16.

17. Francis W. Steckmast, *Corporate Performance: The Key to Public Trust* (New York: McGraw-Hill, 1981), p. 5.

18. Robert Kaiser, "Big Business Moving to Get Off the Bandwagon of Reaganomics," *Washington Post*, March 29, 1982, p. A8.

19. Timothy B. Clark, "Business Behind Closed Doors," *National Journal*, April 3, 1982, p. 597.

20. Kirkland, "Age of Ron," p. 156.

21. "Washington Wire," *Wall Street Journal*, February 10, 1983, p. 1.

22. David S. Broder, "Talk Is Cheaper Than Investment," *Washington Post*, April 18, 1982, p. B7.

23. "A Signal to Business," *Business Week*, May 31, 1982, p. 98.

24. Thomas B. Edsal, "Weakened Business Lobby on the Defensive," *Washington Post*, December 9, 1982, p. D11.

25. Arjay Miller, *How Business Should Respond to the New Pro-Business Climate* (St. Louis: Washington University Center for the Study of American Business, 1982), p. 4.

Chapter 5

1. Richard D. Lyons, "Pension Reform Bill Signed by President on 'Historic Day,' " *New York Times*, September 3, 1974, p. 1.

2. Bruno Stein, *Social Security and Pensions in Transition* (New York: Free Press, 1980), pp. 69–71.

3. Sumner H. Slichter, James J. Healy, and E. Robert Livernash, *The Impact of Collective Bargaining on Management* (Washington, D.C.: The Brookings Institution, 1960), pp. 373–74.

4. Office of Management and Budget, *Special Analysis Budget of the United States* (Washington, D.C.: Government Printing Office, 1983), p. g-32.

5. U.S. Congress, Senate Committee on Labor and Public Welfare, *Welfare and Pension Plans Legislation: Hearings Before the Subcommittee on Welfare and Pension Plans Legislation on S.1122 and Related Bills* (Washington, D.C.: Government Printing Office, 1957).

6. Peter Henle and Raymond Schmitt, "Pension Reform: The Long, Hard Road to Enactment," *Monthly Labor Review*, November 1974, pp. 3–4.

7. Charles Culhane, "Industry, Labor Push Conflicting Approaches to Pension Legislation as Congress Nears Action," *National Journal*, September 9, 1972, p. 1424–25.

8. Bureau of National Affairs, *Daily Labor Report*, June 28, 1972, p. A14.

9. Ibid., May 23, 1973, p. A8.

10. Frank Griffin and Charles Trowbridge, *Status of Funding Under Private Pension Plans* (Philadelphia: University of Pennsylvania, Pension Research Council, Wharton School of Finance and Commerce, 1969).

11. Murray Latimer, "Benefit Security in Private Pension Plans—A Review Article," *Monthly Labor Review*, May 1970, pp. 47–50.

12. Bureau of National Affairs, *Daily Labor Report*, August 6, 1973, p. A9 and October 5, 1973, p. A12.

13. Chamber of Commerce of the United States, *Congressional Action*, May 10, 1973, p. 1.

14. James W. Singer, "New Pension Reform Enacted; Law Gets Mixed Reaction," *National Journal*, August 31, 1974, p. 1318.

15. Chamber of Commerce of the United States, *Congressional Action*, August 16, 1974, pp. 4–5.

16. President's Commission on Pension Policy, *Coming of Age: Toward a National Retirement Income Policy* (Washington, D.C.: Government Printing Office, 1981), pp. 26–28, 31.

17. Ibid., p. 21.

18. Committee for Economic Development, *Reforming Retirement Policies: A Statement by the Research and Policy Committee of the Committee for Economic Development* (New York: The Committee, September 1981), pp. 10–12.

19. U.S. Congress, House Committee on Ways and Means, *The Multiemployer Pension Plan Amendments Act of 1979: Hearings on H.R. 3904,* Statement of Paul H. Jackson on Behalf of the National Small Business Association, 96th Congress, 2d Session, February 19, 1980 (Washington, D.C.: Government Printing Office, 1980), p. 108.

20. Harrison Donnelly, "Employers Seek to Overturn 1980 Legislation to Safeguard Industry-Union Pension Plans," *Congressional Quarterly Weekly Report,* April 3, 1982, pp. 736.

21. "Keeping Up," *Fortune,* February 1977, p. 91.

22. Internal Revenue Service press releases, 1975–80.

23. Pension Benefit Guaranty Corporation, *Analysis of Single Employer Defined Benefit Plan Terminations* (Washington, D.C.: Pension Benefit Guaranty Corporation, 1981), pp. 2–5.

24. U.S. Comptroller General, *Effect of the Employee Retirement Income Security Act on the Termination of Single Employer Defined Benefit Plans* (Washington, D.C.: General Accounting Office, April 27, 1978), pp. i, 5–6.

25. Pension Benefit Guaranty Corporation, *Analysis,* p. 37.

26. U.S. Comptroller General, *Effects of the Employee Retirement Income Security Act on Pension Plans with Fewer Than 100 Participants* (Washington, D.C.: General Accounting Office, April 16, 1979), p. i.

27. Arthur Andersen & Co., *Cost of Government Regulation Study for the Business Roundtable: Executive Summary* (Chicago: Arthur Andersen & Co., 1979), pp. 40–41.

28. Statement of the ERISA Industry Committee before the Subcommittee on Labor of the Senate Committee on Labor and Human Resources, May 19, 1982 (in press).

29. "Rescuing 2,000 Pension Plans," *Business Week,* April 28, 1980, p. 62.

Chapter 6

1. National Commission on Unemployment Compensation, *Final Report* (Washington, D.C.: Government Printing Office, 1980), pp. 38–39.

2. Ibid., p. 191.

3. Daniel S. Hamermesh, *Jobless Pay and the Economy* (Baltimore: Johns Hopkins University Press, 1977), pp. 31–58.

4. U.S. Congress, House Committee on Ways and Means, *Phase III: Proposed Changes in the Permanent Federal-State Unemployment Compensation Programs* (Washington, D.C.: Government Printing Office, 1975), p. 131.

5. National Commission on Unemployment Compensation, *Final Report,* pp. 80–84.

6. American Enterprise Institute Legislative Analyses, *Unemployment Compensation: Reinsurance and Cost Equalization Proposals* (Washington, D.C.: The Institute, 1978), pp. 15–17.

7. UBA, *Advisor,* April 8, 1965.

8. "Review of the Session," *Congressional Quarterly Almanac 1966* (Washington, D.C.: Congressional Quarterly Service, 1967), p. 85.

9. U.S. Congress, Senate Committee on Finance, *Unemployment Insurance Amendments of 1966: Hearings on HR15119, An Act to Extend and Improve the Federal-State Unemployment Compensation Program* (Washington, D.C.: Goverment Printing Office, 1966), p. 268.

10. UBA, *Advisor,* October 21, 1966.

11. Charles Culhane, "Labor Readies Stronger Jobless Pay Plan, Rejects Version Offered with Nixon Trade Bill," *National Journal,* June 9, 1973, p. 824.

12. UBA, *Advisor,* April 1, 1970.

13. Ibid., August 13, 1970.

14. "Jobless Benefits: Major Reforms Proposed," *Congressional Quarterly Weekly,* July 19, 1975, p. 1590.

15. "Will There Be Time for Jobless Pay Bill?" *Industry Week,* August 2, 1976, p. 22.

16. UBA, *Advisor,* May 27, 1980.

17. U.S. Congress, House Committee on Ways and Means, *Administration's Proposed Savings in Unemployment Compensation, Public Assistance, and Social Services Programs, Hearings Before the Subcommittee on Public Assistance and Unemployment Compensation* (Washington, D.C.: Government Printing Office, 1981), p. 104.

18. Ibid., p. 128.

19. UBA, *Advisor,* February 24, 1981.

20. Ibid., August 3, 1981.

21. Eric Oxfeld, "Unemployment Compensation Federal Reform Agenda," *Human Resources Report,* Chamber of Commerce of the United States, August 25, 1981.

22. Paul L. Burgess and Jerry L. Kingston, "Estimating Overpayment and Improper Payments," in National Commission on Unemployment Compensation, *Unemployment Compensation: Studies and Research* (Washington, D.C.: Government Printing Office, 1980), II: 487–88.

Chapter 7

1. Archibald Cox, "The Role of Law in Labor Disputes," in *Unions, Management and the Public,* ed. E. Wight Bakke, Clark Kerr, and Charles W. Anrod (New York: Harcourt, Brace, and World, 1967), p. 632.

2. Ornstein and Elder, *Interest Groups,* pp. 144–46.

3. Interview with Richard Creighton, Executive Director, Congressional Relations, Associated General Contractors of America, Washington, D.C., April 29, 1982.

4. National Action Committee on Secondary Boycotts, "Secondary Boycotts—Construction or Destruction?" 1977, p. 1.

5. Barry Hager, "Labor Lost to 'Intense' Targeted Lobby Effort," *Congressional Quarterly Weekly Report,* March 26, 1977, p. 522.

6. *Congressional Record* (daily edition), October 4, 1977, p. H10558.

7. U.S. Congress, House Committee on Education and Labor, *Labor Reform Act of 1977, Hearings Before the Subcommittee on Labor-Management Relations on HR8410 to Amend the National Labor Relations Act to Strengthen Remedies and Expedite Procedures* (Washington, D.C.: Government Printing Office, 1978), Pt. I: 525.

8. Myron Roomkin, "A Quantitative Study of Unfair Labor Practice Cases," *Industrial and Labor Relations Review,* January 1981, p. 254.

9. Julius G. Getman, Stephen B. Goldberg, and Jeanne B. Herman, *Union Representation Election: Law and Reality* (New York: Russell Sage Foundation, 1976), p. 108.

10. U.S. Congress, House Committee on Education and Labor, *Labor Reform Act of 1977,* Pt. I: 158.

11. Ibid.

12. U.S. Congress, House Committee on Education and Labor, *Report on the Labor Law Reform Act of 1977,* No. 637 (Washington, D.C.: Government Printing Office, 1977), pp. 45–46.

13. Walter S. Mossberg, "Will Carter Tilt the Labor Law," *Wall Street Journal,* August 17, 1977, p. 14.

14. George Meany, "For Working Americans: Time for Justice," *AFL-CIO American Federationist,* June 1978, p. 3.

15. D. Quinn Mills, "Flawed Victory in Labor Law Reform," *Harvard Business Review,* May-June 1979, p. 94.

16. "What Situs Taught the Unions," *Business Week,* April 11, 1977, p. 100.

17. Juan Cameron, "Small Business Trips Big Labor," *Fortune,* July 31, 1978, p. 81.

18. Thomas Ferguson and Joel Rogers, "Labor Law Reform and Its Enemies," *Nation,* January 6–13, 1979, pp. 19–20.

19. Robert W. Merry and Albert R. Hunt, "The Company Line: Business Lobby Gains More Power as It Rides Antigovernment Tide," *Wall Street Journal,* May 17, 1978, p. 33.

20. Quoted in Mills, "Flawed Victory," p. 97.

21. Green and Buchsbaum, *The Corporate Lobbies,* Appendix D.

22. Merry and Hunt, "The Company Line," p. 33.

23. "Business Fights Union Power Grab," *Nation's Business,* September 1977, pp. 21–26.

24. Barry M. Hager and Mary Eisner Eccles, "Labor Lowers Its Sights, Redoubles Its Efforts," *Congressional Quarterly Weekly,* July 30, 1977, p. 1606.

25. Quoted in Jeffrey H. Burton, "Labor Law Reform in the 95th Congress" (Washington, D.C.: Library of Congress, Congressional Research Service), Report No. 79–65E, March 1, 1979, p. 68.

26. Ibid., pp. 79–80.

Chapter 8

1. George P. Shultz, "The Abrasive Interface," in Dunlop, *Business and Public Policy,* p. 13.

2. "Why Some Executives Are Cooling on Reagan," *Business Week,* February 21, 1983, p. 19.

3. Ann M. Reilly, "Business and Reagan: More Blowups Ahead?" *Dun's Business Month,* December 1982, p. 38.

Index

Action Committee on Secondary Boycotts, 120, 121
Ad Hoc Corporate Pension Fund Committee, 78
AFL-CIO, 16, 61, 90, 119, 129
AFL-CIO Building and Construction Trades Department, 85
Albertine, John, 63
Amalgamated Clothing and Textile Workers, 129
American Academy of Actuaries, 81
American Bankers Association, 70, 81
American Business Conference, 13, 29, 40, 56, 60, 86
American Business Network (BizNet), 23
American Council for Capital Formation, 56
American Council of Life Insurance, 81
American Enterprise Institute, 44, 48
American Farm Bureau Federation, 120
American Iron and Steel Institute, 55
American Petroleum Institute, 45
American Retail Federation, 92, 120, 130
American Society of Pension Actuaries, 70, 81
American Trucking Association, 86, 120
Ashton, T. S., 9
Associated Builders and Contractors, 45–46, 92, 120
Associated General Contractors, 45, 83, 92, 120, 122
Association of General Contractors, 45–46, 86, 118, 131
Association of Private Pension and Welfare Plans, 70, 81

Baker, Howard, 141
Bituminous Coal Operators Association, 45
BizNet. *See* American Business Network
Blough, Roger, 36
Booth, Arch N., 23, 24
Boren, David, 110
Broder, David, 62
Brown, William, 104–5
Burns, Arthur, 36
Bush, George, 54

Business and Industry Political Action Committee, 16, 52
Business Council, 13, 22; membership and structure of, 29, 30–31; political ties of, 26; and Reaganomics, 59; relationship of, with Business Roundtable, 31, 35
Business Roundtable, 13, 22, 26; and Business Council, 31, 35; and Carlton group, 56; and common situs picketing bill, 120; and ERIC, 81; and labor law reform bill, 129, 130, 139; membership and organization of, 29, 30, 34, 35–39, 50; and Reaganomics, 59–60; and right-to-work, 119; and UI, 92
Byrd, William, 134

Carlson, Jack, 141
Carlton group, 56, 60–61
Carter, Jimmy, 121, 129
Carter administration, 6, 33
Center for Small Business, 44
Center on National Labor Policy, 49
Chamber of Commerce, 12, 26, 51; and American Business Network, 23; attempted merger with NAM, 23–25; and other business groups, 39, 56; Center for Small Business, 19, 44; and common situs picketing bill, 120; Council for Small Business, 19, 44; Council of State Chambers of Commerce, 92, 100, 108–9; Council on Unemployment Compensation, 92; and ERISA, 74–77, 78, 80, 81; and labor law reform bill, 129, 130, 131; membership and organization, 16, 17–19, 20, 21, 24, 50, 140; and Multiemployer Pension Plan Amendments Act of 1980, 83, 85; and NAM, 15, 22; National Chamber Alliance, 52; National Chamber Litigation Center, 21; PAC, 52; and Reagan administration, 18, 59, 60–61; and right-to-work, 118; and UI, 92, 109, 111, 112; and Wagner Act, 117
Chemical Manufacturers Association, 45
Chiles, Lawton, 131
Committee for Economic Development, 13, 22; membership and structure, 26, 29, 30–34;

Committee for Economic Development *(cont.)*
  Research Advisory Board, 33; Research and
  Policy Committee, 33
Committee for Effective Capital Formation, 56
Common situs picketing bill, 120–22
Conable, Barber, B., Jr., 56
Conference Board, 44, 48
Connally, John, 36, 54
Construction Users Anti-Inflation Roundtable,
  35–37
Coors, Joseph, 48
Corman, James, 108
Council for Small Business, 44
Council for Union-free Environment, 15–16
Council of Small and Independent Business
  Associations, 42
Council of State Chambers of Commerce, 92,
  100, 108–9
Council on Employee Benefits, 78
Council on Unemployment Compensation, 92
Creighton, Richard, 121, 129
Coxson, Harold, 129

Davis-Bacon Act, 46, 62
Day, Virgil, 35
Donahue, Thomas R., 129
Dunlop, John T., 120, 121

Eisenhower, Dwight D., 28
Eisenhower administration, 30
Employee Benefits Research Institute, 49, 83
Employee Retirement Income Security Act
  (ERISA), 6, 67, 74–77, 137–39
ERIC. *See* ERISA Industry Committee
ERISA. *See* Employee Retirement Income Se-
  curity Act
ERISA Industry Committee (ERIC), 47, 81,
  88–89
Erlenborn, John, 132

Filene, Edward A., 27–28
Ford, Gerald, 67, 86, 120–21
Ford administration, 6
Frozen Onion Ring Packers' Council, 45

Georgine, Robert, 85
Greenough, Willian, 82
Gullander, W. P., 16–17

Hale, Randolph, 129
Hamilton, Alexander, 141
Harris, Louis, 141

Hatch, Orrin, 62, 131, 132, 134
Helms, Jesse, 52, 134
Henkel, Paul, 104–5
Heritage Foundation, 44, 48–49
Hill, J. Eldred, Jr., 93

ICESA. *See* Interstate Conference of Employ-
  ment Security Agencies
Interstate Commerce Commission, 9
Interstate Conference of Employment Security
  Agencies (ICESA), 104

Javits, Jacob, 71–72, 78, 132, 134
Johnson, Lyndon B., 31, 71
Johnson administration, 16, 28, 103, 105
Jones, James R., 56
Jones, Reginald, 53

Kamber, Victor, 129
Kenna, E. Douglas, 23, 25
Kennedy, John F., 31, 123
Kennedy administration, 28, 30

Labor law reform bill (1977), 122–24
Labor Law Study Group, 35–37, 119
LaFollette Civil Liberties Committee, 117
Landrum-Griffin Act, 118
Lesher, Richard, 20, 24, 25, 51, 59, 61
Levitt, Arthur, Jr., 40
Long, Russell, 78

McColough, Peter, 82
McHugh, Thomas J., 60
McKevitt, James, 131
Madden, Carl, 20
Madison, James, 9
March group, 35–37
Massa, Clifford T., III, 57
Meany, George, 128
Meese, Edwin, 23
Melgard, Andrew, 80
Milliken, Russell B., 60
Mills, Quinn, 128
Mills, Wilbur, 103, 110
Multiemployer Pension Plan Amendments Act
  of 1980, 68, 80, 83, 84, 85

NAM. *See* National Association of Manu-
  facturers
National Action Committee for Labor Law
  Reform, 129, 131, 133–34, 135

National Action Committee on Secondary Boycotts, 120–21, 130

National Association of Manufacturers (NAM): attempted merger of, with Chamber of Commerce, 23–25; and other business groups, 39, 56; and Council for Union-free Environment, 15; and common situs picketing bill, 120; and ERISA, 71–72, 74, 76, 78, 81, 85; and labor law reform bill, 127, 128, 129, 130; membership and organization of, 12–15, 16, 24, 50; and organized labor, 17; *PAC Manager,* 16, 52; and Reaganomics, 60; and right-to-work, 118; and UI, 92, 111; and Wagner Act, 117

National Association of Realtors, 141

National Association of Wholesaler Distributors, 61

National Auto Dealers' Association, 86

National Chamber Alliance, 52

National Chamber Litigation Center, 21

National Commission on Unemployment Compensation, 98, 113

National Congressional Club, 52

National Conservative Political Action Committee, 52

National Construction Employers Council, 85

National Coordinating Committee for Multiemployer Plans, 85

National Federation of Independent Business (NFIB), 13, 26, 50; and common situs picketing bill, 120; and ERISA, 81; and labor law reform bill, 130; membership and structure of, 41; NFIB-PAC, 41, 43, 52; and other business groups, 39, 56; and Reaganomics, 60; and UI, 92

National Industrial Council, 92

National Industrial Recovery Act, 27, 28

National Labor-Management Foundation, 120

National Machinery and Tooling Association, 130

National Retail Merchants Association, 74–75

National Retirement Association, 130

National Right-to-Work Committee, 47, 118, 129–30, 131

National Right-to-Work Legal Defense Foundation, 47

National Small Business Association, 60–61, 81, 85, 120, 130; membership and organization, 41, 42, 43

New Deal, 27

Newhouse, Neil, 51

NFIB. *See* National Federation of Independent Business

Nixon, Richard M., 23, 28

Nixon administration, 36, 71, 106–7

Norris-LaGuardia Act, 117

O'Neill, Thomas P., Jr., 122

PACs, 10, 51–52

Pension Benefit Guaranty Corporation, 77, 84

Powell, Lewis F., 20–21, 50

President's Advisory Committee on Labor-Management Policy, 71

President's Commission on Pension Policy, 68, 82–83

Public Interest Research Group, 70

Rahn, Richard, 63

Raynes, Burt F., 15

Reagan, Ronald, 20, 31, 52, 54–55, 121

Reagan administration, 7, 18, 57–61, 83, 94, 110–12

Rector, Stanley, 103–4

Retail Tax Committee, 56

Robinson-Patman Act, 42

Romig, Michael, 109

Roosevelt, Franklin D., 13, 27, 28, 30

Sarasin, Ronald, 122

Shapiro, Irving S., 4, 51, 60

Shultz, George P., 34, 137

Sites, James, 24

Small Business Legislative Council, 26, 42

Smith, Adam, 3, 9, 63, 141

Steckmast, Francis W., 59

Stockman, David, 57–58

Supply-side economics. *See* Reagan administration

Taft, William, 18

Taft-Hartley Act, 35, 118

Thayer, Paul, 20

Thompson, Frank, 132

Trade associations, 45

Trowbridge, Alexander, 16, 17, 25

Truman, David B., 9–10

UBA. *See* Unemployment Benefit Advisers

Unemployment Benefit Advisers, 47, 92–93, 103–5, 107, 109–11, 139

Unemployment insurance, 92–93, 103–7, 108–12
United Automobile Workers, 70
United Steelworkers of America, 70

Vanderbilt, William H., 6
van de Water, John, 135
Viguerie, Richard, 130

Wagner Act, 116–17
Walker, Charls E., 56

Walsh-Healy Act, 61
Weinberg, Sidney, 30
White House Conference on Aging, 71
White House Conference on Small Business, 44
Wilkie, Wendell L., 12
Williams, Harrison, 71–72, 78, 132, 134
Wilson, Woodrow, 46
Wisconsin Manufacturers Association, 93

ABOUT THE AUTHORS

SAR A. LEVITAN is Research Professor of Economics and director of the Center for Social Policy Studies at the George Washington University and is a former chairman of the National Commission on Employment and Unemployment Statistics. He has written more than thirty books. Fifteen of these have been published by Johns Hopkins, including *What's Happening to the American Family?* (with Richard S. Belous) and *Working for the Sovereign: Employee Relations in the Federal Government* (with Alexandra B. Noden).

MARTHA R. COOPER, a former Fulbright scholar and author of *The Search for Consensus,* was a research associate at the Center for Social Policy Studies. She is currently a student at Harvard Law School.

The Johns Hopkins University Press

BUSINESS LOBBIES

This book was composed in Times Roman text and Lubalin Graph Book display
by Brushwood Graphics Studio from a design by Susan P. Fillion. It was
printed on S.D. Warren's 50-lb. Sebago Eggshell Cream paper and bound in
Kivar 5 by The Maple Press Company.